To George!

WITH A LISTENING HEART

a Marianist
with a lev shomea'

Εν Χριστω και Μαρια

Best Bw[?] Sm.

Feast of St James
Apostle
7/25/07

With a Listening Heart

Biblical and Spiritual
Reflections on the Psalms

BERTRAND BUBY, SM

ST PAULS

Alba House

Library of Congress Cataloging-in-Publication Data

Buby, Bertrand.
  With a listening heart: biblical and spiritual reflections on the Psalms / Bertrand Buby.
    p. cm.
  ISBN 0-8189-0972-2
1. Bible. O.T. Psalms—Criticism, interpretation, etc.   I. Title

BS1430.52.B83 2004
223'.207—dc22
                              2004012250

Produced and designed in the United States of America by the
Fathers and Brothers of the Society of St. Paul,
2187 Victory Boulevard, Staten Island, New York 10314-6603,
as part of their communications apostolate.

ISBN: 0-8189-0972-2

Printing Information:

Current Printing - first digit   1   2   3   4   5   6   7   8   9   10

Year of Current Printing - first year shown

2005   2006   2007   2008   2009   2010   2011   2012   2013

Table of Contents

Table of Contents

Acknowledgments

This book entitled *With a Listening Heart* is especially dedicated to Professor Eric Friedland, Ph.D., who has been a dear friend and a support in my endeavors, my studies, and my prayer life. Professor Friedland taught Judaics and Hebrew at United Theological Seminary, Antioch College, the University of Dayton, and Wright State University. He has a "listening heart" and a brilliant mind. I have learned much from him in our dialogue meetings and in our times together.

I wish also to dedicate this work to the spiritual leaders of the Jewish community here in Dayton, Ohio, and elsewhere. Among them I wish to mention Rabbi Ira Sud who continued my Hebrew lessons while I was teaching at St. James Catholic High School for Boys, 1956-1960; Rabbi Samuel Fox (emeritus) and now his son Hillel Fox of Beth Jacob Synagogue; Rabbi Jack Riemer, Rabbi Samuel Press, and presently Rabbi Barsky of Beth Abraham Synagogue; Rabbi Selwyn D. Ruslander, Rabbis Joseph Weizenbaum and Howard Greenstein, Rabbi P. Irving Bloom, and now Rabbi David Sofian of Temple Israel; Rabbi Judith Chessin of Temple Beth Or, head of the Synagogue Forum of Greater Dayton; and Rabbi Nochum Mangel of Chabad.

The Dayton Christian-Jewish Dialogue started in 1972 as a lay movement and grew to national and international prominence through the national workshop. The dialogue group consists of almost fifty active members, but it has reached thousands of people through the workshops offered during the past thirty years. It was from the spirit, ideas, images and the themes presented in the dialogue meetings (over 300 of them) and the national workshops that many of my reflections upon a given psalm were developed.

I wish to remember my Marianist Family of sisters, brothers, and brother-priests as well as the lay branches and the spiritual Affiliates of the Society of Mary and the Daughters of Mary. They have shared their spirit, prayers and friendship throughout the years. They have encouraged me to continue writing on scriptural topics. I owe my "listening heart" to them.

I wish to thank Joanne Beirise, who tirelessly worked with me on the manuscript both in format and editing; Eileen Moorman, who helped on reading the proofs and gave valuable insights; and Connie Breen, for her promotion of this project.

My brother Edward James has been a true prayer partner and support in all of my ministries and writing endeavors, and I am grateful for his prayer and friendship.

To Dr. G.J.E. Sullivan, now a venerable nonagenarian, who first introduced me to the original language of the psalms with Psalm 113.

Introduction

B y way of introduction, let me share with you how I came upon the theme, "With a Listening Heart," for this series of reflections on the psalms. One of the members of my congregation told me about a retreat house in Texas run by a contemplative order of women religious. He loved the location and the spirit of silence and prayer there. He then told me that the name of the retreat center is *Lebh Shomea*, the listening heart. (In this book, we will be using a different transliteration of this Hebrew phrase: *lev shome'a.*)

In the Hebrew Scriptures there are two words for the heart, both coming from the same verb; they are *lev* or *levav*. In the biblical anthropology of the psalms the word heart means the very center of the human person. Understanding, intentions, decisions, feelings and emotions are all part of the word *lev*.

The word for listen is *shama'*. This word likewise has many nuances. It completes the human heart in responding to God, for it includes listening attentively, obeying, answering a desire or prayer, understanding and examining something. Hence, it does harmonize with the general disposition of the psalms, namely, to pray them with a listening heart. The word appears 79 times in the psalms which frequently contain the spirit of Deuteronomy which uses the word "listen" some 86 times. Psalm 95:7 captures the meaning of what I am trying to say: "O that today you would listen to his voice."

When I took up the project of writing this book on the Psalter (Book of Psalms), I immediately thought of these Hebrew words and translated them into the title and theme of my writing. Out of a total of 853 times in the *Tanakh* (Hebrew Bible), the psalms use the words for heart 137 times or about 15 percent of its use in the Hebrew Scriptures. The word for heart is possibly the most frequently used word after the names for God. And the *Shema'* (listen) is the great prayer of the Jewish people taken from Deuteronomy 6:4: "Hear, O Israel! The Lord is our God, the Lord alone!" I consider the Book of Deuteronomy to be the heart of the Torah and the psalms to be the heart of prayer. The two words of "listening heart" or *lev shome'a* are not found together in the psalms, but the expression of both Deuteronomy and the term for heart occurs frequently. As I said, I liked the meaning of the expression and now quite frequently use it in my personal reflection and prayer. The more I thought about it in approaching the psalms, I realized that it would be an appropriate theme for writing about them. Hence, the title felt right.

I realized that I had another dimension of experience which would add to the book and that was my work with the Dayton Christian-Jewish Dialogue for over thirty years. This meant that I had prayed, studied, listened to, and celebrated with many of the Jewish people involved in the dialogue. I felt I had many insights and reflections which would fit my presentation of a study of the psalms which would be fresh and interesting. Since I had learned Hebrew over fifty years ago and kept working at reading it in the Hebrew Scriptures, I decided to always work from the Hebrew text in reflecting and researching the psalms for this work. It was a joy to see myself increasing in the vocabulary and thought structures of the psalms as I moved along with each psalm and with each of the five "books" within these psalms.

Introduction

To make sure I was interpreting the psalms correctly I did use about twenty commentaries in order to confirm what I was seeing within the text. The precise and concise information given in the well-known one-volume commentaries were helpful in checking my research and presentation, but I made sure I consulted many other books, too. Nevertheless, I was convinced that by a continual rereading of the Hebrew text I would find what would be my best reward in preparing this book for popular reading. I was convinced that many would appreciate the findings without going into great exegetical details about these psalms and their vocabulary as well as about the variations in the text. I did pay attention to the important insights of the scholars, but rendered them in a readable manner in order to help the reader appreciate the psalms while reflecting upon them or praying them.

Since I am no stranger to writing a personal journal on my own prayer life based on the Scriptures, I thought I could turn to the psalms in this study. I found that a good part of my spiritual and adult life is reflected in the way I pray and think about the psalms. So as time went on I did find that I was very much at home with both my research and my personal prayer seen in each psalm. The constant theme and attitude that I found helpful was to have this "listening heart," a *lev shome'a*.

My love for the psalms was intensified in learning Hebrew from an excellent teacher and linguist, Brother Gerard Joseph Edward Sullivan, S.M. He invited two of the very best students at the University of Dayton to take the course. I was interested, so I became the third in this adventure. Brother gave each of us a Hebrew name. The brightest was named Judah, the Lion of the class; then came the second brightest, who was named the graced one, Yohanan. I was called the "consoler," that is, Menahem. We learned both modern and biblical Hebrew, and memorized Psalm 113. The course continued in the second summer and all three of us were there to enjoy the wonderful creativity and methods of our superb teacher. He kept pushing us to learn and I was challenged by the other two students to keep pace with them while only taking the Hebrew course that summer. Luckily, I was able to do this. Then I was given a teaching position in Chester, Pennsylvania, where I looked up the rabbi at the synagogue, Ira Sud, who eventually would move to Chicago. He helped me with Hebrew and kept me focused on this important language for understanding the Hebrew Scriptures. I was thrilled when some years later I received a postcard from Rabbi Sud from Jerusalem.

In 1960, the religious congregation to which I belong, the Marianists or the Society of Mary, asked me to go to the seminary in Fribourg, Switzerland. There, I was quite fortunate in having one of the great scholars of the Dead Sea Scrolls and the Septuagint, the Dominican priest, Dominic Barthélemy, O.P. I continued Hebrew with him and Johannan and Judah while we even learned how to sing the melodies for the Hebrew text of the Song of Songs. These were a great four years at Fribourg, where my language skills were sharpened and new ones developed while attending classes in Austria and studying in Germany. I was being prepared by my own choices to learn how to read the original languages of the Bible and also to know the principal modern ones used in studying the Scriptures. In 1964 I was given the opportunity to concentrate exclusively on the study of Scripture and to work toward a degree in Scripture at the Pontifical Biblical Institute. This gave me the opportunity to go to Jerusalem on two occasions for three months each. There, I studied both modern Hebrew and biblical Hebrew. My residence was near the great synagogue in Jerusalem, at the nearby Ratisbonne monastery where we read Hebrew before each meal, usually a text from the books of Samuel. I remember going to the House of Abraham where the Dominicans studied with, and under, the direction of some great Hebrew teachers. Those who gathered were taught the Hebrew of the psalms and its meaning. It was really a Golden Age of study for me, as I came to realize later as I began my own teaching career at the University of Dayton in Ohio. This university is under the direction of my congregation, the Society of Mary (Marianists).

Here under the tutelage of Barthélemy and Professor Ernst Vogt my study of the psalms was enhanced. It prepared me for the work that I finally decided to do this past year on the psalms. I was now convinced that the theme *lev shome'a* was appropriate and fit both my research and my prayer reflections in the light of the Dayton Christian-Jewish Dialogue. Both mind and heart were working together in this endeavor, and I gained a real passion for studying each psalm and praying it well.

In my academic arena I had written about Psalm 95 and memorized it for the beginning of my morning prayer each day. It is the invitatory for the Liturgy of the Hours Office of Readings formerly know as Matins. I also prepared an academic response to Doctor Alan Cooper, who was working on the Anchor Bible's new commentary on the psalms that is forthcoming. I offered a new English translation of Psalm 27 and a study of it on the occasion of the silver anniversary of the renowned Dr. Eric Lewis Friedland, Ph.D., my personal friend and advisor for improvement of my pronunciation of the Hebrew texts.

I pray the psalms each day in the Liturgy of the Hours and have done so since the time of my ordination as a deacon in 1963. This keeps me in touch with the prayers of the *'anavim* or the ones totally dedicated to God through the psalms. It consists of at least ten different psalms each day of the week; thus, in a month the entire Psalter is covered. I recently learned that the Coptic monks recite all 150 psalms during their prayer each day! I have a long way to go.

A number of years ago I had tried to write a commentary on the psalms using my personal experience of them, but I was not ready then nor did I have the right theme for doing this. It was only this past year that the theme of a listening heart was the way to approach my writing about the prayers so dear to me that I love with a passion. On New Year's Day, I began the research and study of the psalms that I now offer to you. It soon became evident that I had the energy and passion to accomplish such a work.

Different Literary Types

What are the different literary types or genres of the psalms that we are about to encounter? Here are the types I will mention at the beginning of a psalm. This enables us to focus on the psalm and its variable moods and occasions for prayer.

Hymns of Praise: These psalms are ideal for morning and evening or night prayers. They focus on praising God and extolling God's name. They are Psalms 8, 19, 29, 33, 100, 103, 104, 111, 113, 114, 117, 135, 136, 145, 146, 147, 148, 149, 150.

Thanksgiving Psalms: These express gratitude for favors received from God who is ever faithful and kind in beneficence.

Individual thanksgiving psalms: 9/10, 30, 32, 34, 40 (vv. 2-12), 41, 92, 107, 116, 138.

Community thanksgiving psalms: 65, 66, 67, 68, 118, 124.

Lamentations: These are the most numerous and are powerful emotional expressions of the human heart in many trying circumstances. They are both individual and community psalms:

Individual lamentations: 5, 6, 7, 13, 17, 22, 25, 26, 28, 31, 35, 36, 38, 39, 42/43, 51, 54, 55, 56, 57, 59, 61, 63, 64, 69, 70, 71, 86, 88, 102, 109, 120, 130, 140, 141, 142, 143.

Community lamentations: 12, 44, 58, 60, 74, 77, 79, 80, 82, 83, 85, 90, 94, 106, 108, 123, 126, 137.

Wisdom Psalms: 1, 37, 49, 73, 91, 112, 119, 127, 128, 133, 139.

Liturgical Psalms: These center on worshiping God in the Temple or on a festival: 15, 24, 50, 68, 81, 82, 115, 134.

Trust Psalms: These come from the hearts of those who depend entirely upon God. They are the poor of Yahweh (*'anavim*) for God alone is their security and rock of safety. See Psalms 11, 16, 23, 27, 62, 63, 91, 121, 125, 131.

Royal Psalms: These center on God as king and also on the kings of Judah who have the spirit of David. The latter are seen as servants of God.

God as king: 29, 47, 93, 96, 97, 98, 99.

Kings like David: 2, 18, 20, 21, 45, 72, 78, 89, 101, 110, 132, 144.

Zion Psalms: These speak of Zion, the center of worship in Jerusalem established by David. Zion is called the city of David: Psalms 46, 48, 76, 84, 87, 122.

Frequently one will be able to see that the psalm is classified differently by the scholars. I have depended upon Sabourin, Boadt, Castellino, Schaefer, and Weiser for some of the genres. They, however, do differ on several psalms.

Several Suggestions for Meditating or Praying the Psalms

The psalms are the heartbeat of prayer in the Bible. They are the responses of people who are in love with God. God is in an I-Thou relationship with the ones who prayed and now pray the psalms. The loving-kindness (*hesed*) and fidelity of God permeates each psalm and gives confidence to the psalmist and the ones singing and praying. Both the individual and the community are at prayer in the psalms.

Immediately in taking up a psalm, God is center stage. It does not matter what type of psalm it is, God is always called upon. God is at the heart of the psalms, and the ones who composed them realized that to be totally dependent upon God is at the heart of these prayers. Often this relationship with God is quite emotional and even unusual in its expressions. The strong language sometimes seems offensive to us, but it was not so to those who prayed in some difficult and terrifying circumstances. The strong metaphors and imagery are taken from the everyday religious and social life of a people often under attack, yet who were convinced God would save them. We realize that the psalms are almost 3000 years old; they are not always easy to understand. That is why we need to know their literary type and some of the history behind each psalm.

In a little book called *A Short Dictionary of the Psalms,* John-Pierre Prévost offers seven suggestions for better understanding the psalms. I am simply listing them without their explanations. They are:

1. The psalms are to be experienced as dialogues.
2. They are prayers involving the whole human body.
3. They are meant to be sung to music and even dance.
4. They are expressed in simple, concrete language.
5. They are a deep expression of our humanity.
6. Some are prayers of conflict for us.
7. Help! and Hallelujah are two focal words in the psalms.

I would suggest that you use at least two translations while studying or praying a psalm. This will be both a journey of the mind and the heart, but remember that to experience them, you need to have a listening heart, that is, a *lev shome'a.*

My method consisted in the following steps. First, a thorough reading and study of the Hebrew text while carefully noting the vocabulary, themes, and genre of the psalm. I read over and over again the Hebrew text before going to any translation. Secondly, I collected over twenty important works on the psalms, commentaries and studies. This enabled me to check my insights and interpretations in line with those who researched the psalms. Third, I devoted reflection and prayer time to the psalm and then reflected on the important things I learned and experienced in the meetings and retreats and socials with the members of the Dayton Christian-Jewish Dialogue. My memory came alive through the priming of the psalms and many specific incidents and exchanges were then applied to the psalm I was researching. I was amazed how easily some of these experiences came back and seemed in line with my experience of the psalms.

Though many Christian works have been published on the psalms, I found nothing along the lines of what I was doing. I was convinced this could help those who are dedicated to praying the psalms whether they be Christian or Jewish. My adherence to staying within the bounds of the Hebrew text and then sharing the results of dialogue with Jewish members convinced me this work would be helpful for prayer. I entered into the psalms from a focus on God as God is presented within the Psalter and the synagogue. I opened my heart to each psalm, asking God to give me a listening heart while praying or studying these poems. I encourage the reader to enter into the psalms with a listening heart. You will not be disappointed in hearing the voice of God as David once did, as well as those who followed his expressions of praise and thanksgiving.

I leave you with a blessing given to a community upon reception of a Torah, and I am asking you to apply it as you pray the psalms:

> May your eyes sparkle with the light of Torah [*the Psalms*]
> May your ears hear the music of its words
> May the space between each letter of the scroll
> Bring warmth and comfort to your soul.
> May the syllables draw holiness from your hearts
> And may its holiness be gentle and soothing
> To you and all of God's creatures.   (Siegel, 39)

Abbreviations

ANET Ancient Near Eastern Texts
NAB   New American Bible
NJB   New Jerusalem Bible
NRSV New Revised Standard Version

With a Listening Heart

Psalm 1
ॐ

True Wisdom: *Ashrei* in the Hebrew of this psalm means happy, blessed, or even fortunate. The psalm introducing the whole of the 150 psalms may at the outset of its composition have been coupled with Psalm 2. Even Luke in the Acts of the Apostles seems to be aware of this tradition (13:33). In Jewish tradition David is the one who composed the scroll of psalms, but historical and literary analysis and exegetical studies tell us that the psalms range from the time of David down to the end of the Babylonian captivity and even into Maccabean times (1000-140 B.C.E.). David is said to have composed those psalms that start, as Psalm 1 does, with the word "happy" or "blessed" and usually end with the same word. This actually does happen with Psalm 1 and Psalm 2 which end with the word "happy." So traditions both Jewish and Christian are worth looking into in praying and studying the psalms. Our opening psalm is beautiful in its structure and though it is quite simple in its content, it has a great lesson in wisdom for us. It emphasizes that we must continually ponder over the word of God or even better as the Hebrew indicates, we should "ruminate" and turn over and over again the sacred words God gives us especially in the psalms. This will lead us to choose the right paths and ways in life. God's word is called Torah here in Psalm 1 (verse 2) and this means God's word is revelatory and instructive as given through God's servant David. Meditating and pondering over this word of God enable us to make the right decisions in life and choose the way of righteousness, not wickedness, which is like chaff blown by the wind. We are encouraged to do such praying both in the morning and in the evening. This will result in spiritual happiness and wholeness. Then like a tree planted by life-giving waters we will be nourished, strengthened and rendered fruitful in our actions and words. This imagery is attractive and satisfying to souls which wish to ruminate and ponder over and over, again and again, God's law (Torah) and instruction. Spiritual success is assured in doing this.

Psalm
2
☙

For the first time in a psalm the word messiah or anointed one is mentioned. For us Christians this is an important fact. We must keep in mind that in Jewish circles this word is used only for the king of Israel or Judah. David is called God's anointed one. We Christians, both from our Scriptures and also from our tradition, see this psalm as messianic and referring to what is said about Jesus in the New Testament. This is also emphasized in Christology as well as in the liturgy where we use the psalms as responses to the first reading in the Liturgy of the Word, which may be taken from the Hebrew Scriptures or from the New Testament. The psalm does fit both David and Jesus in their respective roles within the Scriptures.

Psalms are often related to God's enthronement as the true king of Israel; the others are God's servants. Thus the kings then would also be included in the meaning of the psalm. Those who follow David as kings of Judah are especially considered as anointed ones of the Lord. Jesus springs from the royal line of David in Matthew's genealogy and thus is considered a *davidid*. In a recent translation published by the Jewish community there is a suggestion that there are parallels in this psalm in 2 Samuel 7:14 and Psalm 89:27. It so happens that these two passages are considered to be messianic also in relationship to what is said about Jesus in the New Testament. Once again, this makes us aware that the Jewish community is thinking of David and his successors, while the Christian community is thinking of Jesus our savior.

On a personal level, I am moved by the strength of this psalm which shows God as the protector both of the king and his successors. In the psalm God laughs at those who think they are able to overcome the anointed king with their plots and attempts against his life. I am led to think of a passage in our Christian Scriptures where a blind man calls out for help to Jesus saying, "Jesus, son of David, have pity on me." That is also my prayer as I meditate on this psalm. During the Christmas season it also makes sense to me when I sing, "*Venite, adoremus Dominum.*"

Psalm 3

This psalm is a morning praise which is in close relationship to Psalm 4, a night prayer. It is an individual's lament or personal cry for help in time of distress and oppression from one's own people or maybe one's own family. It is filled with emotion concerning the situation the person is facing. This could be David, the king himself or someone close to the king. One enters easily into the heart of this prayer and seeks with the psalmist to find an answer from God whose presence is being felt and called upon for protection. The language suits a soldier or a king who is being pursued even by his own people and family as was the case of David with Absalom. A plot is part of the intrigue of those against the king. The prescript indicates that it is Absalom with his rebellious hoard of miscreants. Even the life of David is threatened. This naturally would explain the deep feelings expressed in the prayer. Just as the psalmist rises from sleep and turns to pray, God also is asked to rise up from sleep and come to aid the one praying. This is very familiar language between God and a human, but it is characteristic of the personal dialogue felt in many of the psalms. What a wonderful relationship between God and the soul to pray in such a personal and confident manner. The song speaks to me when I feel down and out or when I am too tired to do anything worthwhile. God is always there to help me if I but offer such a prayer. I am led to trust in God in all of the personal anxieties I feel and in my disappointments and woes. The psalm is consoling and human in its expressiveness and in its intimacy with a personal God.

Psalm

4

This psalm complements Psalm 3 as an evening prayer or night prayer of David. I was struck by the personal dialogue the writer or composer (possibly David) has with God who is called *YHVH* or *Elohim* (Lord or God). This intimacy of David with God is instructive in its boldness. Confidence and assurance are evident on the part of the one praying. David is resting under the mantle of God. God is addressed five or six times as Lord or God in this short psalm. This shows us how frequently we can call upon God in our needs. This helps us to become aware of the presence of God in our lives. This is a good night prayer which can help us sleep comfortably under the protection of God's loving care. We are able to rest securely without our normal anxieties and worries bothering us. David sees himself at this stage of his life as a righteous and holy person, thus he is able to have such intimate contact with God through prayer. David can be called a just person (a *ẓaddiq* in Hebrew) and a devout man (a *ḥasid* in Hebrew). He recalls the priestly benediction so familiar to his people Israel and offers it as part of this prayer (Numbers 6:25-26ff). This is a perfect night prayer for a soldier or an immigrant or a lonely person when there is little time left in the day. Night comes upon us and we need to have only a short cry or prayer to God at this hour, for we are tired and need to get to sleep and rest for the next day.

Psalm

5

☙

Like Psalm 3 this psalm is also a morning prayer. Once again it is an individual lamentation according to the form and literary critics. I am again struck with wonder at the remarkable intimacy and openness between this person and God. This helps us to form our own prayers and make them intimate and personal with a loving God of peace and calm. God is there for us as a personal friend and protector and companion. This psalm shows us how to have reverence and awe in the presence of God (a gift of the Holy Spirit called fear of the Lord). God is not a power or force in our lives but a person who loves us as a friend. The faith of the Israelite who prays this psalm is strong and pure. This is another lesson in prayer for us. In this psalm the Jewish community uses verse 8 as a beautiful way to pray when entering a sanctuary of the synagogue: "I will bow down toward thy holy Temple in fear of Thee." This is the disposition of a soul truly reverencing God through holy and awesome fear. For me this verse is the most significant one in the psalm. The rest of the verses seem to better fit those involved in political or royal realms with their own peculiar needs in conflict situations. I, however, find myself more in tune with the more emotional and personal elements of this psalm. In a sense I am in different straits than this psalmist, but the words are helpful.

Psalm

6

🙵

This psalm is more personal in its poignancy than Psalms 1-5. It is considered by both the Jewish and Christian communities as one of the seven penitential psalms (6, 32, 38, 51, 101, 130, and 143). They stretch throughout all five parts of the Psalter which imitates the fivefold nature of the Pentateuch. These psalms are excellent for reflection during the Lenten season or while participating in the Sacrament of Reconciliation. The psalm is an individual lamentation. It seems to fit someone who is critically ill yet has strength to cry out to God. Having read this psalm in other languages, I find it quite moving in the Italian translation. This is a good way of studying and praying the Scriptures, that is, reading different English translations or using different languages while reading them. The core or center of the psalm is contained in verses 3-5 which are quite moving and show the circumstances and the anxiety in the heart of the one praying. The Latin for this psalm captures this well: *"Miserere mei, Domine, quoniam infirmus sum; sana me, Domine, quoniam conturbata sunt ossa mea, et anima mea turbata est valde; sed, tu, Domine, usquequo? Convertere, Domine, et eripe anmiman meam, salvum me fac propter misericordiam tuam."* There, in these words, we are at the heart of the penitent and the sick or aging person. If only we could pray in this manner when we are ill or feeling the effects of aging. In knowing people in health care or nursing care centers where people are lonely, ill, and depressed, I believe this psalm speaks with realism. I only hope I can remember this when it happens to me or when in visiting them I offer to pray this psalm with them. In the final verses of the psalm the one facing all these problems comes to some type of spiritual resolution, for God's mercy (*hesed*) is constant, and the praying person comes to realize and thank God for the many graces of healing received throughout this ordeal and other sufferings in his or her life.

Psalm 7

Poetic Justice. This psalm gives us one of the basic themes found in the entire book of psalms, namely, absolute confidence and trust in God our protector. We can picture from the psalm a situation in David's life that is similar to what is expressed in Psalm 7 (cf. 1 Samuel 24). Saul, a Benjaminite and Cushite, hates David because of his success as a soldier in Saul's army. David was winning the favor of the people who considered him a better warrior than Saul, their king. Saul even tries to kill David with a thrust of his spear, but the agile warrior dodges the spear and escapes. David holds no grudge against the king, but the animosity of Saul continues to fester and grow because of his anger and changing moods. These are dangerous tendencies in any leader. The psalm shows us how David may have prayed to God for help in his troubling situation with the king. His inward struggle is reflected. He is a just man who has served his king well, but nevertheless the king hates him. Verse 9 shows us this righteousness of David and is an important key to the psalm: "Judge me, O Lord, according to my righteousness and according to my integrity that is in me." Do we not all feel like David does when we are unjustly treated or even hated by someone? We may not have done anything wrong, but someone calls our integrity into question and we are disturbed by those calumniating us. Our only recourse is prayer to God who knows our inmost thoughts and desires. God also knows our innocence and integrity. Like the conclusion in this psalm, our prayer has to be accompanied by some type of an external act of offering to God to attest to our own convictions about who we really are. Verse 18 is this concrete expression as a thanksgiving offering to God who alone is all-holy and just and who understands that, in this instance, we are innocent.

Psalm
8

A Hymn to our Creator. A verse from this psalm, which magnificently praises God as the Creator especially of humans but also of the whole universe, was placed on the surface of the moon by the first astronauts who landed there. "When I look at the heavens, the work of thy fingers, the moon and the stars which thou hast created: what is man that thou art mindful of him, and the son of man that thou dost care for him?" The fact that the word "moon" is significant and also that the word "man" follows in the next verse are probably the reasons behind the choice of this Scripture. The psalm resonates with three other hymns to the Creator (Psalms 19, 29, and 104). Such thoughts are only possible for one who is in deep contemplation of the Creator and creation. This wonder is so compelling that it leads us, the readers, to pray or to contemplate in a similar way. The marvels and wonders of the vastness of the universe and the world are so mind-boggling that contemplation is the only response to the one who created all of this reality called the world and the universe. The hymn is based on the priestly tradition of creation given in chapter one of Genesis especially as it comes to the apex of creation, human life or ADAM (Genesis 1:26-27). I had a similar experience of the power of the universe as a young boy of 13 or 14. I was returning home around midnight after selling newspapers at the Westinghouse plant. It was lucrative because that was the last shift and both the men and I waited for the midnight whistle. I had to shuffle the papers into their hands as deftly as a quarterback does in the NFL (National Football League)! As I hurried home up a side alley I looked up at the stars and the skies and suddenly was overwhelmed with wonder. I was in the presence of someone or something sacred as a child of the universe. I felt awe and warmth and had a sense of belonging to this presence. Yes, even in the verses that follow, the psalm harkens back to the babies or nurslings whose babbling and prattle is part of the mystery of God's creative hand which can offset the proud and haughty (see verse 2). St. Irenaeus once exclaimed, "The glory of God is man [and woman!] becoming fully alive." This psalm is a reflection on such an experience leading us to praise God as Creator. The contemplative inspired writer of this psalm has to end the song just as he had started it: "O Lord, our Lord, how glorious is thy Name" (verses 2 and 10).

Psalm

9

୫

Both lamentation and thanksgiving from an individual are found in this psalm. At once the prayer starts out praising and thanking God, but as we continue reading it we find there is conflict and tension because of the oppression from people and warriors in the kingdom. The introductory thanksgiving does show us that the one praying has confidence in the protection of God and that the difficulties that are being faced can be overcome because God is the Lord and Protector of the nation. The individual could be King David; the opponents, his own people and soldiers. Perhaps, by reading this psalm with the background of 2 Samuel, chapter 8, one may be able to capture the flavor and feelings of the composer.

God is described as a judge who is just and who will condemn and vanquish the enemies of the king and the faithful people. The lowly, the poor, and the humble are mentioned as being of concern to the one who offers this prayer. These "poor" of God (the 'anavim) depend solely upon God in all their needs and in the state of oppression they feel from powerful overlords and the rich. The humble may also be classified with the 'anavim or the "members of the community who were faithful to God even under trials." Baeck states, "The word poor is a word which the Bible pronounces with devoutness and with reverence, as if in holy awe" (cited in Cohen, 23). In the New Testament in the Gospel of Luke, we see that Mary is among the 'anavim in her song of praise (the Magnificat). Jesus also reminds us in the Sermon on the Mount that "Blessed are the poor in spirit for theirs is the kingdom of God" (Matthew 5:3).

Psalm 10

A Cry for the Oppressed. Our psalmist is aware of the wicked scoffing of some arrogant leaders displaying their greatness and self-sufficiency. These types take it out on the poor, the orphan, the widow and the weak. The one offering this prayer is quite upset about this behavior. The high-handedness and the cruelty of the oppressors are crisply developed in the first 11 lines of this psalm. The resolution of such oppression comes only in the last nine lines of the psalm. In some translations one could be led to believe that these people are also atheists, but it does not seem likely that there is an authentic atheism anywhere within the Bible. Nevertheless, some translations do say, "There is no God." What is happening is that the arrogance and self-confidence of these wicked ones lead them to be in contempt of God, saying that God has no interest in human affairs, nor does God thwart their evil machinations. The ones who are relishing this type of practical atheism inflict great pain on the ones who trust in God, and the psalmist is voicing his anguish to God. I, too, feel his frustration and pain as he offers this prayer in the Temple. This type of oppressor or oppressors is similar to a lion waiting to pounce on its prey. The psalmist identifies himself with the poor and the humble (again one of the 'anavim) and does know and realize that God does care; God does see what is happening. What is so painful for the psalmist is that these people are from his own homeland and even from his own community. Eventually, God will answer this prayer and refute the wicked ones. Fortunately, as the psalm comes to a close, a direct cry is made to God to rise and observe what is happening. Then the prayer surely will be heard and answered — but when? Only in God's time.

Psalm
11
ૐ

By this time, you and I realize how frequently the name of God is mentioned and called upon in the psalms. They are totally God-oriented or theocentric. In the present psalm the most sacred name of God (*YHVH*) is mentioned explicitly five times within its seven lines. In this prayer we see a person who reflects upon an impending attack on the city of Jerusalem. He is deciding whether to listen to his advisors or not. He decides to put all his trust in God and not in these counselors who are encouraging him to flee to the mountains as do the birds. This coincides with some of the events in David's life when he fled for his life from the rage and jealousy of Saul. The one praying realizes that the sacred name of God indicates God's presence in the tent or sanctuary. The name Yahweh can mean that God is ever present and goes before the people in their needs and concerns, or that God simply is the one who exists and causes existence in all of creation. The sacred name is closest to the verb in Hebrew which means "to be or to exist." The human respondent to God who is sincere and observant is called the righteous one (*zaddiq* in Hebrew). This person is aware of the presence of God in all that he does and of course in the observance of God's precepts. The word for the just one or *zaddiq* appears 139 times in the psalms. It refers also to the relationship which that person has with God and to the saving justice of God given to all such persons. The psalmist concludes that salvation will and does come from God and not from the advisors who give faulty or timid advice. This is a good lesson for us about the process of how to decide and discern. We, too, need to address God in prayer and remain confident in the presence of God in our decisions.

Psalm
12

☙

This is a community lamentation about the sad state of affairs under King David in his kingdom of Israel-Judah. It seems that the complaint is voiced by a devout person (a *hasid* in Hebrew), who for the community expresses a need to experience honesty and truth from those in leadership positions who possess smooth tongues and are proud of themselves and their words. The psalm possesses a good number of words that are used twice, indicating a certain style of the composer. Perhaps, he does this deliberately to offset the double-tongued smooth talkers who also have, in his words, a double heart (another way of expressing their duplicity). The problems of society then have an answer for them through an oracle from God. God will rise up and offset what the liars and slippery-mouthed are doing to the poor and the needy. God always hears the cry of the poor and needy (the '*anavim* and the *evyonim* in Hebrew). God's truth is absolute; like silver seven times refined in the fire, they are also totally pure. We notice that in verse 6, God answers the prayer of the psalmist: "I will set the needy and the poor in safety."

Psalm 13

This psalm is an individual's lamentation. But it is not negative, for one of the characteristics of the psalms is that they are a dialogue with God. This psalm is an example of an individual who commiserates with God and four times asks when will my troubles and sorrows end. How long, O God, must I wait? Through his prayer he moves from despair to hope. Martin Luther in reflecting on this psalm says, "Hope despairs and yet despair hopes." In dialogue with God, the psalmist addresses God personally as *YHVH-Elohim*, that is Lord-God. The amazing prayer is answered, for God evidently responds to this person's persistence in the request — as we said, four times the person praying asks, "How long, O Lord, how long?" At the end of the prayer the person sings and praises God, for he or she receives the favor of God's answer.

Song and dance are part of the way the psalms were presented to God in the Temple. Eighty-seven of the psalms have instructions to the music leader. If we have experienced the psalms as sung we catch the mood, movement, and emotion of these prayers. Singing them is praying them twice. The theme of hope is strong throughout the Psalter. This virtue appeals to our heart and its desire to be in dialogue with God with some difficult issues, maybe different from our psalmist, but similar, too. God listens and deals with us bountifully and soothes our minds, hearts, and bodies when we enter into such conversation with God.

Psalm 14 ৡ

This is both an individual lamentation and a wisdom psalm. Wisdom is within the fabric of this prayer, and many of its lines and ideas are repeated in Psalm 53. We have already seen in Psalm 1, our introduction to the Psalter, of what wisdom consists: namely, doing the will of God and choosing the right paths in life. We are to choose good over evil at all times and bear fruit at the streams of life-giving waters. However, the psalmist realizes that there are few who seem to choose this right way of living in the presence of God and observing God's precepts. The foolish person thinks that God is not at all involved with our lives. This is the meaning of the foolish statement, "There is no God." It is practical atheism, not full-blown atheism. We have seen that there is no true atheism in all of the Bible. What is happening here is that the fool (naval) is conjecturing that God does not intervene or even care about what we do. So, let us be self-centered as a fool and go for the gold! Apparently, for the psalmist, many in Israel are thinking this way, or, if not in Israel, all the nations think this way. This makes God out to be the greatest fool, and those doing God's will the most foolish among humans. The witless ones lack true wisdom and do not realize how foolish such thinking is. They devour the poor (the *'anavim*) as though they were eating bread. Will God put up with all of this nonsense? No, the psalmist reasons, for God is the refuge for the poor, the *'anavim*. The composer realizes that God will rescue the poor, so the ending is a hope-filled prayer that the people of Israel will be delivered; therefore they should exult and rejoice, for deliverance will come from Zion, God's holy city of Jerusalem (Psalm 14:7).

Psalm 15

This psalm is among the favorites of many who pray the psalms, together with Psalm 23: "The Lord is my shepherd...." It also has similar content to Psalm 24:3-6; Isaiah 33:14-16; Micah 6:6-8. This psalm can help us in our personal and communitarian spirituality, for it puts us into the presence of God as did the original holy people who prayed it while approaching the Temple and house of God in Zion, Jerusalem the holy city. Its introductory verse leads us to also ask, "Lord, who can stand in your presence? And how is this possible?" The answer is given us by either the priest who is answering the question or possibly the composer. We are encouraged to keep all of the precepts and commandments of God especially those dealing with our relationships with one another. A wife and a husband are also included in this way of living and dwelling in the presence of God in their daily lives and in their relationship to one another. "The Talmud remarked that the

613 commandments of the Pentateuch (Torah) are summarized in this psalm, meaning that their moral purpose is here crystallized" (Cohen, 35). "O *Adonai* (Lord), teach us how to love our neighbor as ourselves" (Leviticus 19:18). It is said that David restricted the 613 commandments of the Torah to eleven; Isaiah to six; and Amos and Habakkuk to one. Our psalm has the same spirit.

Psalm 16

Martin Luther's opinion about the introduction to the psalm or the inscription is that it is a "golden jewel." And so it is for the reader or the one praying this song. The content is filled with optimism and joy. It is a hymn of confidence and of joy throughout. It lifts up our spirits because we realize happiness is a good gift from God and we can tap into it through our prayers and especially this psalm prayer. One famous scholar, Father Mitchell Dahood, S.J., who studied the psalms through the background of the Ugaritic tablets found at Ras ha Shamrah (which feature a northwest Semitic vocabulary and narrative that is a substratum for the Hebrew language), senses that the one offering this prayer is a convert from the religion of Canaan which seemed to have a belief in the afterlife. This is carried over into the psalm as it winds down to its conclusion; hence, this may be the first psalm to indicate a belief in personal resurrection. There is a wonderful ease with which this person communes with God — almost with the enthusiasm of a convert! This makes death seem to be an obstacle that can be overcome through this union with a personal God. The hope and joy are stronger than the bonds of death. The psalm is a wholesome expression of a person who has found himself and found God. Mind, heart, and body are integrated in this prayer of a righteous one who may be a Canaanite or a Levite (one who served in the Temple and one from the priestly clan of Israel). Personally, when I pray this psalm, I feel motivated and uplifted by the thoughts expressed in such a joyous and confident way.

Psalm 17

"Hoping against hope!" A psalm of individual lamentation: the inscription says this is a prayer of David. This is also said of Psalms 86 and 142. It makes us think of the time when Saul the king was pursuing David in the desert of Maon (1 Samuel 23:25f). At night David cries out in prayer to God to justify him for he definitely is innocent and considers himself as only a loyal servant of Saul. He is, however, surrounded and pursued by the army of Saul in the desert, in the mountains, and even in open places. He feels as though a lion is ready to pounce on him as prey. Anxiety and pain inveigh him; he is fatigued and restless. This is seen especially in verses 7 and 8. God will protect him just as one protects and shields the pupils of one's eyes or as an eagle gently protects its young and carries them on its wings. Images from nature are present in the psalm that depict both the protection but also the threats that menace the loyal servant of Saul. The enemies of David are not praying to God in this fashion nor will their offspring. David prays that God will somehow punish them for what they are doing unjustly to him and his men. His situation is like that of a trapped animal. He desires to see the face of God, for only then will he be at peace. Perhaps, in this psalm there is thus a thought about life with God after death which seems to be so

19

near in the circumstances David undergoes. Do we not some-times feel such oppression and opposition in our lives? We can learn how to deal with it from this psalm.

Psalm 18 ☙

"Thee will I love, my strength and my tower" is a hymn by Johann Scheffler trans-lated by John Wesley (1703-1791). The He-brew inscription for this majestic psalm at-tributes it to David when he was pursued by Saul and by other enemies. There is a paral-lel passage in 2 Samuel 22 which contains the same psalm. Which was written first? No one knows for sure, but there may have been an earlier manuscript from which both writings borrowed or copied. To enjoy this psalm, it is best to consider it as an integrated thought of David rather than breaking it up into three different themes as do the literary critics. Wieser favors the unified approach and has the best reflective interpretation that I found among the many. For me this psalm is a marvelous retelling of the life of David dur-ing some trying circumstances he faced. The word "life" comes to mind and I associate it with the symbolism of the number for the psalm: 18. This corresponds to the eighth and tenth letters of the Hebrew alphabet and is equivalent to the word *ḥayyim* in Hebrew which means "life." You are probably familiar with the toast at a wedding, "*le-ḥayyim*... here is to life, your life!" David's life is transparent in this psalm. His name means the beloved of God. He certainly is that, as well as being the beloved of the Jewish people among all the kings of Israel. David's prayer rings true and comes from a heart in love with God who is a tower of strength, a fortress, and a rock for him. The psalm also fits the covenant theme which David harkens back to in the

Sinai and Exodus experiences. The psalm thus becomes alive in the liturgical cult of the Temple after David. Its first and last lines are like bookends offering us, if we have a listening heart and an eagle's eye, a library for prayer marked with grace and salvation history. The psalm is one of the most vibrant and life-giving ones in the Bible. Maybe that is why we have two versions of it in the inspired Hebrew Bible.

Psalm 19

This psalm has two parts which are complementary. First, there is a hymn to creation in the expanse of the universe which is the handiwork of God. Then in the second half of the psalm there is the inner universe of the soul seen through the Torah that God has revealed through Moses. In the first hymn, the poet combines both metaphors and myths about the sun which is similar to a bridegroom coming from the bridal chamber who is also a warrior who runs to victory throughout the day into night. The hymn to creation differs from Psalm 8 which emphasizes humankind in creation. Here the emphasis is on the overwhelming vastness and beauty of the universe and the sun which runs its circuit like a bridegroom-warrior. The second part of the psalm concentrates on the Torah and its principles and precepts. Here we enter the soul's universe as guided and directed by God, the bridegroom of the soul. It is just as vast and wonderful as the universe of stars and planets, sun and moon. The commandments of the Torah are also food for the hungry soul. The philosopher Immanuel Kant may have been inspired to write the following words after reading this psalm: "There are two things that fill my soul with holy reverence and ever-growing wonder — the spectacle of the starry sky that virtually annihilates us as physical beings, and the moral law which raises us to infinite dignity as intelligent agents." The psalm ends with a beautiful thought about meditating with the heart on these wonders: "Let the words of my mouth and the meditation of my heart be acceptable before Thee, O Lord, my rock, and my redeemer." Amen.

Psalm 20

This is a royal psalm. But it is also a psalm that opens us up to the wonderful sounds of music in the Temple on Mount Zion where almost like a concert in a church the power of music enhances the meaning of the words and the celebration of the people. Temples, churches, and sacred places beckon us to sing joyfully, confidently, and harmoniously to the Lord, the King of the universe, the King of kings. We know the psalms were accompanied by all sorts of music and with musical instruments like the trumpet, the cymbals, the horns, drums, and flutes in all sorts of arrangements as the inscriptions tell us. Today's psalm seems quite appropriate for celebrating the enthronement of God as king during the festival of the New Year. Perhaps, earlier this may have been a psalm with intercessions to God by people through a priest or prophet of the Temple before the king went to battle, but with time, it came to fit the festivity of enthroning God as king in their hearts and especially in the Temple in Jerusalem or — as it is called here — Zion. Despite the many human elements in a psalm that seem to come from the individual who composes, sings or prays the psalms, there is the Person to whom they are all addressed, and that is God. God is the one who is the great King (Psalm 95:3). In our present psalm, the first five verses are asking God, who is in the Temple seated above the cherubim, to help his servant the king of Israel. God helps him in the present, not in the future. It is interesting that the word used for victory is the same word used for salvation. The name of Jesus stems from the same radicals in the word for salvation, *yeshu'ah*. We all can sing out, "Long live the King!"

Psalm 21

"Our heart's desire" — a royal psalm. Both the king of Israel and God are extolled in this psalm. Verse 8 acts as a hinge that keeps both the king and God together in the choirs that alternate in the singing in the Temple. The verse says, "For the king trusts in the Lord (*YHVH*). Through the faithfulness (*hesed*) of the Most High he will not be shaken." In the first part the choir sings about the lifelong blessings the king will receive from God: blessings of honor, majesty, and power (verses 2-7). A spirit of joy and celebration permeates the entire psalm and it reminds us of a coronation ceremony for a king. The choirs alternate and the priest or psalmist recites or chants verse 8. In the second part of the psalm, God is celebrated as the real King behind the throne. The words are so generalized that this could be used for many celebrations and not just one occasion. God is the one whose presence is acknowledged in the Temple at a precise moment in the song. We, too, can join in singing God's praises by concentrating on the last verse which is an inclusion with the opening verse. In this way, we are given our heart's desire while praying this psalm. Amen.

Psalm
22
☙

One of the most profound meditations on the sufferings of a just person or on the corporate identity of Israel as the Suffering Servant of God is offered for our reflection in this psalm. Jesus is ending his life on the cross while using the opening words of this prayer, "My God, My God, why hast Thou forsaken me?" Even the Jewish commentary states, "A Christological intention has long been read into this psalm…" (Cohen, 61). It seems likely that the most Jewish gospel has taken this psalm and used it as a framework for the narrative of Jesus' death upon the cross (Matthew 27:35-46). In the New Testament, this psalm is mentioned 24 times within ten of the inspired writers among the 27 of the Christian Scriptures. In the post-apostolic age (100-200 C.E.) it is cited and commented upon more than any other psalm, and in the patristic writings it is by far the most cited psalm (300-700 C.E.).

In Judaism the corporate image of the Suffering Servant of *YHVH* (the Lord, God) is called to mind in the spirit of Deutero-Isaiah (chapters 40-55). Thus for both traditions this psalm is most profoundly prayed. In it the very soul of the psalmist is bared and becomes transparent for the community of believers whether Christian or Jewish. I was personally touched by the depth of the anguish released and by the ultimate trust in God that it inspires while reading, praying or even studying it. It touches the mystery of suffering and death. It is related by Christians to the death of Jesus; it probably resonates with the survivors of the Holocaust (Shoah) and its horror and despair. Both Jew and Christian profit by meditating on this prayer that can only be explained as a divinely inspired masterpiece.

*Psalm
23*

☙

This is one of the most well-known psalms, loved by people all over the world. It has been sung and recited at liturgies and worship services the world over. It is also used at services for Christian burial and does bring comfort to those hearing and praying it on such occasions. Yet, in its original social location it may have been said by one who remained in the Temple after a celebration of one of the great feasts. There he is most thankful to God and is enjoying moments of peace and tranquillity. He expresses thanks and is enjoying the warmth of God's presence. Communion with God is apparent as we read the psalm slowly and enter into this prayer. Images of the life of a shepherd (God) stimulate his imagination, but he knows in his heart that it is the real presence of God that calms him and stills his heart. God restores and refreshes him and us (verse 3); God indicates safe paths for our journey through some rough places and difficult times. Thus the psalm is meant for us, the living, even though we frequently hear it in a funeral home. Jacob, our patriarch in the faith, who spoke of "the God who hath been my shepherd all my life long" (Genesis 48:15) is also in tune with the spirit of our psalm. I believe we all can thank God for those moments where we sensed the divine presence in chapels, synagogues, or in our homes. God's love and guardianship are to be treasured when we pray this poetic psalm.

Psalm

24

A liturgical hymn of greeting in the Temple (Mount Zion). Pilgrimages are important and exciting for deepening one's faith with others. We remember a sacred place and we experience the presence of God in the people and the event. Our psalm is connected with a pilgrimage experience to the mount on which the Temple of the living God *YHVH* stands in the holy city of Zion (Jerusalem). The introduction recalls that God is the Creator of the universe and all that is in it: the heavens, the earth, yes, even Mount Zion. We know that this psalm was said on the first day of the week and thus it fits the story told in Genesis 1 about the first day of creation. The pilgrims who ascend the mount are desirous of being purified and made holy as they approach the sacred site. In a chorus they voice this desire: "Who can enter the holy place of God's dwelling?" A priest responds that those who have ritually clean hands (no bribes), those with pure intentions, those who honor God's sacred name, and those who do not speak falsehoods to another person. Then the gates of the Temple are opened up and they approach the presence of the one who resides in the Temple. The glory of God (*kavod*) permeates the sacred place and is captured in the final lines of the psalm. It is similar to the experience of the great prophet Isaiah. There the theophany of experiencing the presence of God takes place and the walls of the Temple resonate with "Holy, holy, holy is the Lord God Almighty" (cf. Isaiah 6:1-9).

Psalm
25

An individual lifts his/her soul up to God. This is classified as an individual lamentation or prayer. It made me think of it as a good psalm before spiritual direction with a friend or a priest. In such sessions the person seeks guidance in leading a good and integrated spiritual life. Prayer, ministry, community and personal concerns are shared and listened to by the spiritual director. The person who prayed this psalm is one who is close to God and aware of God's guidance in life's concerns and issues. God is seen as offering loving-kindness, friendship, and mercy. It is a good image of God, one that is not too small! In the spiritual journey we recall faults and failings from the past, not in order to feel guilty, but to thank God for how far we have come. The right paths are now sought and God is at the heart of our prayer. God is there with a listening heart (*lev shome'a*). There are thoughts shared that are filled with wisdom (verses 8-14). The foundational strengths of the covenant are present both for the individual and the community to which he or she belongs. Exodus 34:6 is recalled: "The Lord, the Lord, a God merciful and gracious, slow to anger and abounding in steadfast love and faithfulness...."

As we wrestle with similar thoughts, the words of St. Paul confirm the depth of the prayer we offer to God through this psalm: "We know that all things work together for good to them that love God" (Romans 8:28). We join with our psalmist praying, "Remember, Lord, Thy compassions and Thy mercies; for they have been from of old" (Psalm 25:6).

Psalm
26
֍

This is a very emotional psalm in which an innocent person, perhaps a Levite who attends to the Temple rituals, invokes God to vindicate his innocence. The rituals and the recalling of the precepts of the Torah seem to stem from a similar idea found in 1 Kings 8:31-32. The protestation and the water ritual around the altar are calling upon God who is ever faithful and true to exonerate the one who may have been unjustly accused. This person is sensitive to the presence of God near the ark of the covenant in the Temple and wishes to always have the right to be there. God's goodness and mercy are hoped for. As we read this prayer and take it to our listening hearts we notice that the poem is carefully constructed in a series of matching verses, for example, the beginning verses match those at the end, then the next matches the next to the last. In the center are the key verses (especially verse 8). The Levite cries out, "Lord, I love the house where you dwell, the tenting-place of your glory." Similarly, we are encouraged to dwell in the presence of God whether in a sanctuary of a synagogue, a temple, or a chapel or church. We, like the Levite, desire to remain with the Lord in this sacred place, on this sacred ground.

Psalm

27

A psalm of two different moods. This psalm consists of two distinct parts. The first six verses are a prayer of great confidence in God's loving protection. In many details of thought and language, it is similar to Psalm 23, "The Lord Is My Shepherd." Yet, God is not presented as a shepherd. The Jewish understanding of the psalm is that it is done by the same poet and is just one psalm. The differences in the two parts are simply presented as a change in the mood of the one praying. We, too, go through this in ordinary life and in our own way of praying. The synagogue uses this psalm as a daily prayer in their sixth month when they think of preparing for the New Year and for the Day of Atonement (*Yom Kippur*). God is first imaged as light and salvation. The psalmist is centered on the cult of the Temple and desires to live in the house, the tent, the Temple of the Lord — all meaning the same sacred place in this psalm. The prayer is answered and the poet-psalmist then offers a thanksgiving prayer. Then the mood changes in verse 7 till the end of the piece. Here I feel the guilt and introspection of the one praying. It acts eventually as a catharsis similar to the Sacrament of Reconciliation. We, like the psalmist, recognize our sinfulness and cry out to God for help and forgiveness. We yearn to see the face of God. We wish to relieve ourselves of this guilt feeling, this anxiety, and we desire to experience the loving-kindness and mercy of God. Again our listening heart is asked to take courage and to wait patiently for the forgiving glance of God. It does this twice in the last line — hope, wait on the Lord.

Psalm 28

There are 37 psalms which are called individual lamentations. Our Psalm 28 belongs to this literary genre. We can easily identify with these psalms since they are so personal and emotional. With our psalmist we can cry out to God as in verses 1 to 5. I think we often feel the same as the one praying in this psalm. We cry out and it seems that God does not hear us. Maybe God, too, needs to have a "listening heart." Sometimes our episodes in life are stormy and troublesome; this leads us to lament or, perhaps, better said, to complain to God. We need to speak and God needs to listen to us. We ask with the psalmist that God not be deaf to our outcry (verse 1). Whether the opposition or the enemy be one or many, we are hot and bothered about the situation. Then as we pray we seem to get an answer from God who was listening all the while. We, like the poet, then turn to a prayer of thanksgiving which often is also the pattern in the lamentation psalms. Verses 6-7 are a hymn of thanksgiving. The final verses of this psalm are a later addition which makes the piece adaptable to a public worship of God or a liturgical celebration in the Temple. Some experts claim that this part of the psalm may actually go back to the time of the first Temple in Jerusalem and maybe to David himself. That would be 3000 years ago! And yet the prayer is still so much in tune with our times and our personal complaints to God. The word "anointed" is found in this last part and hence that always was used in reference to the king who resided in Jerusalem. God then is a shepherd to this king and to the people.

Psalm
29
🎵

What a magnificent description of a storm! And this may be one of the oldest psalms, possibly transforming a Canaanite hymn into a praise of *YHVH*. There are many similarities to the Ugaritic hymns in their structure and vocabulary. This psalm definitely helps us appreciate the power of God in nature. Many people are in awe at a beautiful sunset, making them appreciate the beauty of God's creation. This hymn does the same for the devout Israelite who discovers the power of God. We are so centered on God through this storm which is overwhelming. God is *YHVH* (the holy one who is, the glorious one). Within the 11 lines *YHVH* is named 17 times. God is at the heart and center of this thrilling experience of the storm with lightning, thunder, rain, and wind making all of nature tremble. Even the cedars of Lebanon, even the mountain named Sirion (Mount Hermon). The cattle, too, writhe and prematurely give birth because of the disturbance of the storm. The psalm reminds me of a great *Gloria in Excelsis Deo* sung at the Mass with full voices and instruments. God's glory (*kavod*) is extolled through this psalm. The word *kavod* which is used for the glory of God occurs 151 times within the psalms out of 200 uses within the Bible. As this psalm ends we are brought into a peaceful realm. It ends with the word *shalom* or peace. We are ready for the Sabbath rest.

Psalm 30

This personal psalm of thanksgiving reminds me of a citation in the *Christopher Notes*, a pamphlet put out by the Knights of Columbus: "It is better to light one candle than to curse the darkness." The Jewish people chose this psalm for commemorating the rededication of the Temple in 165 B.C.E. This came to be known as the feast of light or *Hannukah* and it occurs during the season when we Christians light up Christmas trees. The word *Hannukah* appears in the superscription to this psalm and shows that the original personal prayer has been made a part of the public worship and celebration of the Jewish people. It was probably also a victory over the "abomination of desolation," Antiochus Epiphanes, who had placed his statue in the Temple.

The psalm is a thanksgiving hymn of someone who was near death because of a serious illness. It is a psalm that can help us when we are ill or when we suffer from cancer and hope for its remission. Apparently, this person did have his illness taken away by God and now he offers his song of thanksgiving in the Temple. In looking at the contents of his prayer we discover that *YHVH* is mentioned eight times; *YHVH* is also called God, once, and then the pronouns referring to both titles number seventeen! The prayer is totally God-centered. The prayer starts with a lifting up of mind and heart to God, and God is extolled from on high for God has healed and restored to life the one who was grievously ill. Yes, as this poet says, "God's favor is for a lifetime" (verse 6). And "O Lord, my God, I will give thanks to Thee forever" (verse 13).

Psalm 31

Scholars claim that this psalm is made up of many other passages from the psalms and that it is not a logical presentation on the part of the poet who has assimilated the other psalms so well. His mode of prayer is not a logical presentation to God, but a series of exclamations and prayers of petition that spring from the heart. And the heart has its reasons that logic does not comprehend. Prayer is not a logical process but an open communication with God who is a personal friend to whom even our "sweet nothings" mean so much for it is the language of love. The psalm and our prayers do not have to be logical. This inspired psalm shows us that great prayer comes from our heart with its emotions and sighs. We can pray with passion. Jesus cited this psalm as he died: "Father, into your hands I commend my spirit" (see verse 5 and Luke 23:46). Stephen, the first martyr for Jesus prays in a similar fashion: "Jesus, receive my spirit" (see Acts 7:59). The Church has used this psalm as the regular responsory in night prayer or compline at the end of each day of the week.

This psalm is a prayer of faith of the heart. The psalmist comes to realize that his personal guilt stems from a lack of total trust in *YHVH*; once he realizes this, he comes to his senses and he is healed. Then thanksgiving comes into his prayer and it is expressed in public in the Temple. The final verse of the psalm again stresses that prayer comes from a "listening heart": "Be strong, and let your heart take courage, all ye that wait for the Lord" (verse 25).

Psalm
32

A thanksgiving psalm for compunction of the heart. This was the favorite psalm of St. Augustine and his later disciple, Martin Luther, who also said it was one of the four Pauline psalms (51, 130 and 143). These belong to the seven penitential psalms of the ancient Church (6, 32, 38, 51, 102, 130, 143).

I found that Weiser got to the heart of this psalm in saying, "The peculiar quality and permanent value of the psalm are to be found in the realism of its presentation, which makes us sensitive to the true significance of conscience" (282). This psalm has a thanksgiving section (verses 1-7) and a wisdom section (verses 8-11). This prayer contains a remarkable insight and description of the workings of our conscience when confronted with our faults and sins and how we often try to hide these sins from others and even from God. We hope that they go away and that we forget about them. God, however, is never deceived and restores us to loving communion once we realize the truth and confess our guilt. I have experienced all of this while examining my conscience and going to the Sacrament of Reconciliation whether in a communal service or in a private confessional situation. The psychological description is so realistic that I consider this psalm as an excellent preparation for reconciliation and forgiveness. This is especially helpful when I want to hide my sins from everyone, even God.

Both the Jewish and Christian commentators merge in agreement on the interpretation of this psalm and they both unite with my personal experience of confession in the traditional practice within the Catholic Church. The struggle and honesty within this prayer makes me thank God for the grace of divine forgiveness whether it is obtained directly or through the sacrament. Surely, "Blessed is the person whose transgression is forgiven, whose sin is covered."

Psalm

33

🜊

"Sing a new and joyful song to the Lord." This psalm is classified as a hymn and in praying or reading it one can see that musicians would be very pleased with it. All of the sounds and the voices are resounding around the walls of the Temple in Zion, Jerusalem. Instruments are mentioned: a ten-stringed harp and probably a four-stringed lyre. We also know they used tambourines and drums and, of course, the loud but well-tuned full voices of the choirs inside. It also is described as a new song to sing with gusto to the Lord (verse 3). Though I am not a musician, I do love to sing the psalms with my brothers and sisters in our chapels of the Marianist congregation. I enjoy this particular psalm because of its upbeat tempo and its jubilant quality. There are three thematic parts to this singing. First, the beautiful Hebrew words which are descriptive of God's attributes are voiced: righteousness, loving-kindness, justice, and peace. These, of course, are part of the ethical tradition and gift of the Jews to all of us. Secondly, God's act of creation taken from Genesis 1 is chanted and the power of God's word is praised (verses 6-9). Thirdly, the wonderful presence of God in the Temple is accented through God's watchful and piercing eye(s). This is the divine providence of the Creator who is ever watchful over the people of Israel. God's sovereignty is part of the melody among us (verses 14 and 18). I was struck by this sentence from the Soncino Hebrew commentary: "From this rare verb (*hishgiaḥ*) the rabbinical term *hashgaḥah*, 'Divine Providence' is derived. It governs all the inhabitants of the earth, not only Israel" (97). Like our own choirs which belong to a church or synagogue, this psalm is sung by the community of believers in the Temple and it gives to everyone who joins in a real sense of belonging to God's people whether we be Jew, Christian, or Muslim.

35

Psalm 34
♱

This psalm has both an individual's thanksgiving hymn and also a portion that is an instruction in wisdom. Both parts belong to the same composer who unites them with the theme of great trust and hope in God who is ever faithful. The poet is also community minded, for he invites them to join in praising God and also in listening to words of wisdom. Verse 12 starts the wisdom section and addresses the listeners who are youthful and are worshiping with him in the Temple. The poet also uses the alphabet to make his psalm attractive to the participants. He does seem to have some trouble in keeping with all 22 letters of the alphabet in Hebrew. He tries to recover the letters, but they seem misplaced! The psalms are very human in content and formulation. The important message given to us today is that humble prayer offered to the Lord (*YHVH* translated as *Adonai* or Lord) is what is important because the Lord is so worthy of such praise from us. As one of the poor of *YHVH*, that is, as one who is totally dependent on God for his peace and personal welfare, he continues his prayer. It is similar to what Mary will say in her song of praise called the *Magnificat* (Luke 1:46-56). This is especially true of verse 2-4 in the psalm and the first part of Mary's hymn where she too is evidently one of the poor of *YHVH* (that is, one of the *'anavim*).

As I read verse 9, I was aware that we use this for a Communion meditation song and actually discovered that the early Church also used this in preparation for receiving the Eucharist. The verse is beautiful: "O taste and see that the Lord is good; happy are those who take refuge in him" (verse 8). It has been pointed out through archeologists that verse 13 of this psalm is the same as a verse found in the tomb of Pharaoh at El-Amarna: "Which of you desires life, and takes delight in

prosperous days?" This shows the influence of Egyptian wisdom sayings upon the people of Israel. Transformation and
inculturation are part of the mystery of revelation seen in the
psalm.

Psalm 35

A prayer in times of persecution; an individual's lamentation with similarities to the
painful sufferings of Hosea and Jeremiah.
This emotional prayer is one of the longest of
the lamentation psalms of which there are 37
individual lamentations among the 150
psalms. Within this psalm symbols of warfare are given, but this is a metaphorical use,
for the poet really sets up an atmosphere in the judgment court
of God whom he hopes will vindicate him from the slander and
lies of his former comrades and friends. What is called a *riv* or
court judgment seems to be the real situation of the one praying. God is the judge and the accused one brings his case before God. The *riv* continues throughout the psalm after its initial appearance in verses 11, 23, and 27. The military symbols
show how strong are the verbal attacks of the enemy, once his
friends.

In reading this psalm, I sensed the great anxiety and depression the poet experienced. From such a dark and dismal
mood only vindication from God can bring him back to some
tranquillity and peace. One who is depressed does not need to
be taunted, but his enemies do this with the dramatic "Aha,
Aha," inflicted upon him (verse 21). We well know how long it
takes to come out of a deep depression, for this affects our entire person and our well-being. The victim presents seven
strong declarations against his oppressors before the court of

God and then adds in the second part of the psalm seven inter-cessory imprecations against them. He has to win his case or else he is totally devastated. We feel the depth of his misery in his use of the word "destruction," *shoah* which in Hebrew is the very word used by the Jewish people for the Holocaust. This word appears twice in verse 8 and once more in a verbal form in verse 17. This led me to feel even more the anguish of the poet and the hurts he endured from those whom he visited and even prayed for as though they were his brothers. Fortunately, as in most lamentation psalms there are thanksgivings offered to God for the expected or realized deliverance. I was helped in understanding this psalm from advice from a leading liturgist who told me to look at Psalm 22. To this may be added Psalm 7, both of which are individual lamentations with a similar theme.

Psalm 36

This psalm is filled with wisdom and yet it is also a lamentation from a devout believer in God. It is best to consider the psalm as a unit even though in a literary sense it shows two different types of psalm genres. Taking the final form of the inspired Scriptures is always a good way of responding to them in faith and with a "listening heart." I look at the psalm as depicting a form of our struggle with temptation. What seems successful in this world is not always morally the best choice for us, but it is attractive. Our psalmist struggles with this same problem. In fact, sin or transgression is immediately presented in a personified way as a prophetical oracle offering its tempting words and suggestions to follow the wrongdoers. As we approach verse 6, the psalm changes dramatically into praising the good attributes of God that are consistently mentioned in the psalms, namely, God's justice, loving-kindness, holiness, and righteousness. In the light of the contrasts between part one and part two we have something similar to the wisdom psalm, Psalm 1, which opened us to a reflection on the one who is blessed for following the right path and the one who is driven like chaff for following the wrong paths of life. How do we choose right over wrong, life over death? How can we discern the difference between sin and its darkness and the light of life given by God? It is by our focusing on who God is and seeing the attributes the psalms give to God (*ḥesed* = loving-kindness, *mishpat* = just judgment, *zedaqah* = righteousness).

I discovered that Islam in its beautiful calligraphy frequently has a design in which God is shown with 99 attributes! We do well to meditate on God's glory in these superlative attributes and gifts; then temptation to choose evil will not be so attractive. Arthur Weiser, the great scholar of the psalms has this to say about our psalm: "This psalm is a beautiful and living testimony to what faith is capable of attaining when, notwithstanding everything, it takes the risk of siding with God" (306). As he winds down his prayer the psalmist discovers true wisdom and makes the right choice as he reflects on the differences between evil and good. Verses 9-10 are central to the core reflection: "In thy light do we see light."

Psalm 37

An antidote for murmuring. The priest-lawyer Tertullian described this psalm as the "Mirror of Divine Providence." If so, this mirror happens to be the wisdom figure, the guru or the sage who has advice for us when we wonder why bad things happen to good people and good things seem to happen to bad people. We are hearing the words of a teacher and one who is experienced through the passing of the years. He considers himself an old person now and wants to share his moral insights as to how we should look at life's challenges under the providential eye of God. He tells us to wait for the Lord and to be patient and not to fret (don't we have enough of these fretters?). Nor should we murmur or be agitated about the success of those who seem to us to be wrongdoers. His words are similar to the wisdom of the Hebrew Scriptures in the Book of Proverbs and in Ecclesiastes (Qoheleth) who is the "preacher." I like the way Weiser sums up the psalm: "It is a question of the vindication of the practice of religion in man's everyday life, and that vindication takes the form of giving pastoral counsel of a didactic nature" (315).

Another theme running through the psalm is the gift of property or land to those who are God-fearing. We know that the Land is the cherished name for the present state of Israel (which is referred to as *Ha-Arez*, the Land). The motivation is ancient as seen in Deuteronomy and in this psalm (verses 3, 9, 11, 22, 29, and 34), and is probably meant in the use of the word "heritage" in verse 18.

As in some wisdom psalms the author creates an acrostic or alphabetical development of ideas. Sometimes they seem a bit forced or contrived to make an acrostic poem, but it shows the didactic style of the poet. This teacher keeps showing us traditional wisdom which consists in trusting in God: "Trust in the Lord and do good" (verse 3). He also encourages us to be patient and to wait and things will change for the better: "Resign thyself unto the Lord, and wait patiently" (verse 7). We are encouraged to do good: "Depart from evil and do good; and dwell forevermore" (verse 27). The final verse is a summary of the whole psalm.

Psalm
38
☙

Mitchell Dahood produced a famous study on the psalms by tracing certain Hebrew words and expressions back to Ugaritic, an ancient northwestern Semitic language that was deciphered through the discoveries made at Ras Shamra. This enables scholars to clarify some of the more obscure passages in the Hebrew Scriptures. Dahood has done this for all of the psalms. He gives this succinct summary of our psalm 38: "An individual lament; the psalmist is affected by a grave disease. The common belief that illness was a punishment for sin was an unexcelled opportunity to the psalmist's enemies, ever eager to slander, to speculate on the nature of his guilt" (234). There is no doubt that the one who is speaking out in prayer to God is a bona fide sinner. His personal sins lead him to confess openly to God with the realization that sin has brought about his grievous illness. Some scholars speculate it was leprosy or some form of uncleanness, but we have to remember he probably is praying in the Temple! His only hope for some form of relief, at least for his inner self, can come from God who does forgive sins. His anxiety is extreme and intense and in 17 of the 22 verses he openly speaks of his sinful condition. He is not bothered that his friends ridicule him or even gloat over his condition. He is directly concerned about his communion with God and how only God can relieve his anxiety by forgiving his sins. He cannot be bothered with listening to his former friends and neighbors; he is totally focused on God's presence; he is openly admitting all of his sins in a most sincere manner, probably only equaled in Psalm 51.

I was personally touched with this outpouring of his heart to God and his absolute honesty in confessing his sins without blaming anyone else. It is a marvelous example of repentance for me. I think of the Confiteor which has the words, "Through my fault, through my fault, through my most grievous fault." The psalm does have similarities to the plight of Job except unlike Job this person is guilty and admits it at once. His only salvation and healing is through the mercy of God. His last sigh sums up his prayer: "Make haste to help me, O Lord, my salvation" (verse 22).

Psalm
39
🍂

An elegy from a Hebrew psalmist. As I pondered over this wonderful psalm I realized it was an elegy. It reminded me of my favorite elegy, that of Thomas Gray called "An Elegy in a Country Churchyard." The psalm, of course, differs in that the psalmist concentrates on his own inner thoughts and not on the people who have been buried before him. His inner struggles with mortality and his unworthiness are evident in the two equal parts of this poem. The first part is his own soliloquy in verses 1-7; then his personal prayer is seen in the last seven verses. As I read verses 4 and 5, I sensed a lot of my own emotion joined to his as he releases the thoughts of his heart in an outward cry: "But my sorrow increased; my heart smoldered within me. In my thoughts a fire blazed up, and I broke into speech: Lord, let me know my end, the number of my days, that I may learn how frail I am." The psalmist has laid aside his personal rules of self-restraint and while shattering his scruples breaks out in a bold prayer to God. His approaching death brought about by a serious illness is too much to keep to himself; he needs to shout out his complaint to God and does. In releasing this we are able to notice how he has passed through the three forms of Jewish prayer: first the prayer of silence; then an outcry from the depths of his heart; and finally the wonderful gift of tears as prayer. The Talmud states, "From the day the Temple was destroyed, the gates of prayer were locked; but although the gates of prayer were locked, the gates of tears remained unlocked." I was led to think of Jesus in the Garden of Gethsemane as he prayed with sweat and tears and nervous trembling, "Father, if you are willing, remove this cup from me; yet, not my will but yours be done" (Luke 22:42) and Hebrews 7:7: "Who, in the days of his flesh, when he had offered up prayers and supplications with strong crying and tears unto him that was able to save him from death, and was heard in that he feared...."

Psalm 40 ☙

A thanksgiving and a supplication. This psalmist has a sense of belonging to the great assembly, the name given to the faithful participants in the cult and worship ceremonies in the Temple on Mount Zion, Jerusalem. He leads us into his delight for the covenant rituals and the consolation and help he has received from them in the past. He appreciates both the letter and the spirit of the laws governing the offerings made in the Temple. His psalm mentions the rituals of sacrifice, offering, burnt offering and sin offering, and then while respecting them also shows the true spirit behind them which consists in a listening heart, that is, obedience to the God of compassion and fidelity. This attitude transforms both the sacrifices offered and the person offering them. It also serves as a new song which edifies the congregation and the Levites in the Temple. His act of thanksgiving is an appreciation for the graces of salvation and healing he has received in the past. We can easily see this psalm then as an example of salvation history in action. He himself had been delivered by God from the pit of tumult and from former sin or illnesses. Thus, after his community-centered act of thanksgiving, he can turn to a new supplication to the God of mercy and love. The psalm makes perfect sense as a unified prayer despite the two different modes expressed within its verses. We also are able to notice that he borrowed from Psalm 70:2-6 and from Psalm 35:4, 21, 26f. Do we not do the same in some of our prayers when we return to a well-known and cherished prayer we learned earlier in our lives? These passages easily come to mind as we present our prayer today.

Christians started using the psalms found in the Hebrew Bible as early as the second century. They had nothing similar to them in their collection of hymns found here and there in the epistles of Paul. Surely, we all are aware that the inspired writers of the New Testament cited the psalms in their works when they focused on Jesus as Lord or Messiah. Today's Psalm 40 was taken up in the Epistle to the Hebrews 5:5 where verses 7-9 of the psalm are applied to the spirit with which Jesus responded to God. In this he was not unlike the one who wrote the present psalm.

Psalm

41

🜍

A confident prayer in God's faithfulness to the covenant. Some of the psalms are difficult to categorize or classify according to the methods of the literary critics and those who study form criticism. Our psalm under consideration has three different strains within it: wisdom, individual lamentation, and thanksgiving. Perhaps, that is why some scholars simply call it a psalm of confidence. I join them in this perception. We also have the ending of verse 13 which is called a doxology — a praise of *YHVH*, the favored name for God in the first of five collections in the Psalter. Psalms 3-41 are in the Hebrew tradition called the psalms of David, even though we know he composed very few of them. Nevertheless, because of his ability to compose and play during the time of King Saul, these psalms are named after him. In a sense, then, he influenced later composers; hence, David is an appropriate name to associate with the psalms. As I said, this is a psalm of confidence and trust, for this seems to be the golden thread throughout its verses which unites all of the other "strains of music." M. Dahood sees the psalm going back to the time of the monarchy under David and it seems to reflect the betrayal of one of David's friends named Ahitophel who joins Absalom, David's son, in a revolt against David, the true King (2 Samuel 15:12, 31).

Verse 9 is so connected to betrayal that all four gospels use it to describe the betrayer Judas Iscariot (Mark 14:18; Matthew 26:23; Luke 22:21; John 13:18, 17:12; Acts 1:16). Interestingly, both Ahitophel and Judas hang themselves after realizing their crimes (2 Samuel 17:23; Matthew 27:3-10). Probably, you and I have experienced betrayal in some form or another in our lives; it is so poignant an experience that it is hard to forgive and forget those who have betrayed us. This psalm helps us to face our own sins of betrayal and those of others and to forgive ourselves and those who have sinned against us. The psalmist has a wholehearted trust in God who is merciful and forgiving. He pleads for God's help in overcoming his own sins and those of his oppressors. In the wisdom-like verses he prays, "The Lord delivers them (us) in the day of trouble" (verse 1). We pray with the psalmist, "O Lord, be gracious to me; heal me for I have sinned against you" (verse 4). We started this psalm with a blessing on the poor; we end it blessing God with high praise in a doxology. Confidence exudes from this psalm.

Psalms 42, 43 ❦

Two psalms in one song? In my estimation, one of the Levites, a descendant of Korah and one of the musicians of the Korahites who composed a number of psalms, meant these two psalms to be sung together. Scholars move both ways, but the refrain (*ritornello*) present in both Psalm 42 and 43 is the same and is used three times within the 17 lines of the psalms. There is a longing and yearning for the one chanting this psalm to return to the Temple on Mount Zion in Jerusalem. The Levite is exiled to far-off Hermon in Syria where the waters of the mountain flow into the Sea of Galilee and then from that sea into the river Jordan.

These psalms start what is known as the second book of the Psalter or the Elohist psalms. *Elohim* is the preferred name for God in this collection (Psalms 42-83); *YHVH* is the chosen name for God in the first collection known as the Davidic collection. The name *Elohim* (God, or Most High God) will occur 210 times in this second collection, *YHVH* occurs only 45 times and is translated as Lord (*Adonai*). In the rest of the psalms *YHVH* is named 584 times; *Elohim*, 94 times.

The Korahites composed the following psalms (42, 43, 44-49; 84, 85, 87, 88). Our psalm is called a *qinah*, a more reflective piece with lengthier strophes and developed imagery. The psalm is recognized as such by the inscription or introduction given it by the scribes of the psalms. Undoubtedly, the family of Korah were talented composers and musicians as well as chanters.

A beautiful image of a hind cautiously searching for water appears. The sleek and nervous deer keeps stretching its neck to find some water in the dry land. This captures the longing and yearning of the psalmist who compares himself to the hind as he searches to find the Temple and, within it, the God of the living. He is so far away from Mount Zion in Jerusalem. How he would like to be on pilgrimage to the sacred Temple and join the people of God there. Nostalgia, burning desires, great feelings and devotion are evident throughout the psalm which matches the beauty of its imagery in Psalm 23. Our own prayer is enhanced by entering into this psalm and putting all our desire for God into it. We need to develop passion in our prayers. Like the psalmist we then would cry out, "My soul thirsts for God, for the living God" (verse 2).

The refrain within these two pieces is the same and it is this *ritornello* which unites them as a unified song: "Why are you cast down, O my soul, and why are you disquieted within me? Hope in God; for I shall again praise him, my help and my God" (Psalm 42:5,11 and Psalm 43:5). This refrain unites the three phases of the psalm: lamentation, reason for the song or the cause, and finally the prayer seen in Psalm 43. The psalmist desires to see and experience the presence of God (*Elohim*) in the Temple. His haunting melody and devout reflective plaint helps us feel and pray with him. Three times, he returns to the heart of his prayer, "Hope in God; for I shall again praise him, my help and my God."

Psalm 44 ॐ

A national hymn of lamentation. The Jewish tradition places this psalm during the reign of King Hezekiah, who probably was the holiest king the nation ever had. He reigned in Judah 715-687 B.C.E. It is he who made great reforms in the cult and also established the celebration, with solemnity, of the Passover. In this psalm we hear the king and his people reciting a national lamentation. Ironically, the country that is attacking them is Assyria and this form of lamentation originated there as early as 2050 B.C.E. One sees a similar structure in the lamentations that originated in Sumeria.

In our most difficult moments or during a time of national crisis or war, we turn to God in our needs and many who are not religious-minded show up in a synagogue or a church or a mosque. During these times we reflect on the past favors and graces God has bestowed on our country through God's merciful and magnanimous acts (*mirabilia Dei*). We recall how we managed to survive and come through a terrible war or national calamity. We Americans can think of the Civil War of the nineteenth century that decimated the nation and divided the North from the South. In our psalm, the first nine verses do such recalling, remembering how "God was on our side." But we do lament that this is not the case now and we are again facing a war or a national calamity. This is what the next lines do in this psalm, namely, verses 10-26. Like Hezekiah feeling as though he were a caged bird, so we, too, are complaining about our oppressors. We do tend to gather and pray as a community at such times (just think of how our country was united in the weeks after the terrorist attack of September 11, 2001). This seems to be a worldwide situation today and many storm heaven hoping to be helped by God. Like the psalmist we need to recall what is said in the first part of the psalm and then compose a profound and devout prayer to the God who can save us: "Rise up, come to our help. Redeem us for the sake of your steadfast love (*ḥesed*)" (verse 26).

Psalm
45
ॐ

A royal wedding love song. This is one of the ten royal psalms (2, 20, 21, 72, 89, 101, 110, 132, and possibly 18). A very gifted com- poser of songs, probably from the family of Korah, prepared this with great enthusiasm and love for the king and his bride. He takes such great pride in his work that he shares it with us in verse 2: "My heart is stirred with a choice subject and I say: My work is concerning a king; my tongue is the pen of a ready writer." The fact that this may be a secular love song for the occasion of the king's wedding re- minded me of the beautiful secular songs that are sometimes chosen for the prelude music to a wedding. How could this psalm then get into the inspired Scriptures? Probably, not un- like the Canticle of Canticles it was allegorized into the covenant love relationship between God and the people of Israel. This psalm was also taken up by the author of the Epistle to the He- brews to speak of the messiah as Jesus Christ (see Hebrews 1:8- 9).

In the speculation of the scholars several kings of Israel and Judah are suggested: Ahab as king, Jezebel as queen, for she was from Tyre which is mentioned in the psalm, verse 13; or Jehoram and Athalia, whose mother was from Tyre; Solomon is also named because of the relationship to Hiram from Tyre through the queen from Egypt. All of this is speculation and it is best to take the psalm as it is for the occasion of a king's wed- ding without naming that king since the psalm does not. Since the messianic character is suggested both in the Jewish tradition and the Christian tradition, it would seem that it would be a *davidid* or a king from Judah and not from the northern shrine. If I were asked to choose a king by name, I would select Solomon. In the song the great gifts of the king are praised: his military prowess, his justice, his magnificence, and his mercy. The psalmist also turns his poem and song to the queen (verses 11-16) and encourages her to turn away from her attachment to her former homeland and focus exclusively on that of the king. The psalm also has a promise and blessing on the king and queen in their progeny who would continue the lineage and be blessed by God. Finally, we learn from a scholar of the psalms that Psalm 45 is the only example in the whole of Israelite psalm poetry of a true hymn to the king (Mowinckel, 74).

Psalm 46

A hymn of Zion, a hymn of confidence in God. Martin Luther has captured the spirit and heart of this psalm with his own hymn, "A Mighty Fortress is Our God." Confidence in God exudes throughout the verses of this Temple hymn sung by the Korahites. We have seen how their compositions are more reflective and how they use imagery in a powerful way. This psalm is no exception. We see the use of a refrain throughout the three strophes of the psalm. Rather than agree with scholars who say the first use of the refrain seems out of place, I see it as an inclusion or a bookend type of literary technique that links the very opening line with the refrain. The psalm does not mention the word Zion, but it focuses on the holy city and its community at worship. It has a striking use of the name *YHVH* in verse 8 which recalls the Emmanuel prophecy of Isaiah 7:14 (*YHVH Sabaoth* is with us = Emmanuel or God is with us). In fact, this psalm has similar vocabulary and imagery as the classical priestly prophet Isaiah. Isaiah is the prophet who mentions Zion up to sixty times while the psalms do so some fifty times. The strophes show God present and the congregation confident in the tremendous power of nature that causes destruction both on the sea and the land (verses 1-3). The next strophe emphasizes confidence and trust in God when the raging of the nations against Israel takes place; once again the refrain comes through, "The Lord Sabaoth is with us." And in the last strophe which looks to the ultimate judgment and victory of God over all (an eschatological image), there too the confidence expressed in the refrain is heard and sung by the assembly. Keep in mind that the following verses are expressive of this confidence and form a *tour de force* (verses 1, 3, 7, and 11). Weiser has these impressive insights in summing up the psalm: "This inward assurance that flows from man's total surrender to God confers on the psalm the distinction of a song of songs of that faith which confidently faces every kind of danger because it carries with it the unshakable certitude of the victory that overcomes the world" (73-74).

Psalm 47 ♓

A royal hymn dedicated to God the King. This is an upbeat psalm composed by the combined talents of the Korahites, Levites and musicians of the Temple who can be considered the Mozarts of their day! The psalm is a classical hymn which offers us the simple structure of an introduction through the use of a call to shout out jubilantly to God; then a motivation, and finally the body of the song. This psalm offers this structure in two parts balanced with exquisite simplicity and continued enthusiasm. I enjoyed reading and praying this psalm because of the positive and uplifting expressions offered in its verses which were put to music for the Temple choir and the people. The jubilant clamor and the lively sounds of the music indicate the greatness of God as king who is celebrated on the occasion of the New Year festival of the covenant and the enthronement of God.

Yes, God is the king not only of Israel but of all the nations. The people of Israel, however, are the ones who inherit this privilege of serving God the King because of their allegiance and lineage from Abraham who taught them to believe in God.

Within this psalm the command to sing out jubilantly is given five times and the center of this piece probably indicates the ceremony of the carrying of the ark to the sanctuary and there sensing the presence of God abiding above the mercy-seat with the cherubim offering homage. Verse nine reads, "God sits above his throne."

In praying this psalm, I easily recognized the structure of a hymn and saw the balance of part one (verses 2-6) with part two (verses 7-10). I also was led to reflect on the use of *YHVH* for God's name in verses 3, 8, 9, and 10. Normally, *Elohim* is used for God in the second collection of psalms called the elohistic Psalter. Next, I noticed the frequent use of the title king for God or images connected with regal majesty. Though other psalms are used for the celebration of the Feast of Christ the King, this one would be most appropriate. The psalms used for the feast are 23, 93, and 122.

Psalm

48

᭢

A hymn to holy Zion. This psalm sings and celebrates in the cult of the Temple of Mount Zion the greatness of *YHVH* who powerfully protects the city of Zion. His dwelling place is in the sanctuary where the ark of the covenant is placed. This song is similar to an epic which encapsulates the wonder, the awe, and the majesty of God who is king over Israel. The presence of this king extends to the surroundings of the holy city of Jerusalem even to its towers and walls. Hostile potentates are overwhelmed at the fortifications of the city and at the presence of so powerful a God. They flee.

As I ponder over this psalm, I realize that I need to put it in a liturgical and sacramental context if I am to enter into the heart of it. Yes, again a listening heart is the key to this psalm. Though some try to place a specific historical context to it or even an eschatological perspective, it is rather the "eternal now" that is being sung and celebrated in its verses. There is probably a specific Hebrew ritual implied in the psalm like walking around the city in pilgrimage on the covenant festival and possibly on the part of the Levites walking around the altar. Our pondering is not to be only for ourselves but is to be shared with the younger generation who also must have a listening heart towards the sacred sanctuary called Zion and the great presence of God within its Temple. As we move through the verses, we see that the great ships heading to or coming from Tarshish in southern Spain, are shattered by the storms and the raging sea. God, however, protects the people from all of this rage of nature just as God protects them from the onslaught of mighty armies from the north. At the end of the psalm God also battles death in a similar fashion to the mythic Baal battling death (*Mot* in verse 15).

Since this psalm is composed by the creative poets and musicians called the Korahites we see there are other subtle images like the mention of the four corners of the earth where God is also present: north, verse 2; east, verse 8; south, verse 11, and west, verse 14. (These are indicated by the play on words in the Hebrew text but not necessarily seen in our translations.) Zion thus is at the center of the world because it is there that God executes judgment and justice.

I am reminded of how important sacred architecture, sacred space, and sacred music are in centers of prayer like chapels and churches, synagogues and mosques. When these are carefully and beautifully designed, the presence of God surrounds us and envelops us in our worship of the King of Kings.

*Psalm
49*

A wisdom psalm from the Korahite musicians. In reading and meditating on this psalm one smiles. Why? Because the expression, "You can't take it with you," comes to mind. It is not that easy, however, for the psalmist who composed this song did so only after profound and long periods of reflection.

He then presents it as his own riddle or proverb. He informs us that this is a *mashal* (a proverb, a riddle, a metaphor, an insight). The use of the words that explain his understanding are given in the plural which denote profound wisdom and deep insight. A popular Hebrew commentary tells us that "wisdom in the Bible corresponds to moral philosophy; understanding is enlightenment upon a perplexity of human experiences" (Cohen, 152).

After the mention that the psalm is the work of a son of Korah, the next four verses describe his wisdom song and how it came about: "I will turn my attention to a problem, expound my question to the music of a lyre" (verse 5, NAB). Entering immediately into his "problem" he demonstrates that both the rich and the powerful, the poor and the wise, suffer the same consequences as humans: both die. His own fear is allayed by this thought: he experiences peace through his meditation. He ends the first part of the dialectic with the refrain that will end the psalm: "Mortals cannot abide in their pomp; they are like the animals that perish" (verses 12 and 20). Verse 15 is the most perplexing and possibly the most profound statement made in this sung meditation. It can mean that death is the leveler for everyone, but the wise may expect a longer life or at least peace of mind in having figured this out, while the wicked or unwise never catch on to the riddle of life which always ends in death. There is the possibility that a hint of eternal life is present in this enigmatic verse, namely, that God will redeem the ones who are wise and take them up from the power of Sheol (the underworld). Were not Enoch and Elijah "taken up" to a life different from Sheol? We do not know whether this interpretation was in the mind of the composer. Most early psalms do not speak of the afterlife or eternal life with God. What we do know with either interpretation is that there is a confidence and hope expressed by the psalmist in what he has discovered as the riddle of life. We know that this psalm is recited in the house of those who are mourning. Finally, this psalm made me, as a vowed religious, think of a traditional spiritual exercise we used before Vatican II called a "preparation for death." It was as sobering as this psalm may have been for the people who lived during the time of its composition. To sum it up, "You can't take it with you."

Psalm
50
ક

This psalm is considered both as a prophetic instruction from God (*YHVH*) and as the liturgy celebrating and calling forth fidelity to God (*YHVH*). As a prophetic exhortation or oracle from God it can become a learning experience for those who are attentive to God's voice and who have a "listening heart." This psalm is attributed to Asaph or the liturgical descendants of this great composer of sung psalms for the Temple. Psalms 73-83 are introduced under the name of Asaph. Once again the psalm fits the liturgical celebration of the covenant probably at harvest time during the Feast of *Shavuot* or the Feast of Pentecost or Weeks, for it happens seven weeks after Passover.

The spirit is similar to the Book of Deuteronomy which centers on the covenant. Deuteronomy 33:2 may have been the source for our psalm's inspired text: "The Lord came from Sinai, and rose up from Seir unto them; he shined forth from Mount Paran, and he came with ten thousands of saints. From his right hand went a fiery law upon them." God is a holy and righteous judge who holds court with his people, both those who are faithful and those who are not. Those who have failed in keeping alive the spirit of their covenantal commitment are arraigned before all of creation and all of the holy ones (perhaps the righteous and also the messengers of God called angels). Weiser states clearly, "The point of the whole psalm is the powerful experience of man's encounter with God and the conclusions which are to be drawn therefrom" (394).

The introduction identifies God in a unique, threefold way: the mighty one, the judge, and the gracious one. This is God. God, God the Lord has spoken. After the theophany based on Deuteronomy (verses 1-6), the next strophe shows that external ritual sacrifices of animals are being offered, but the

fidelity and trust of those offering them are not visible; the spirit
is lacking (verses 7-15). Then the crimes that account for such
superficiality are put forth by God: thievery, adultery, and slander. These are the three commandments which we would name
the sixth, seventh and eighth commandments. God as judge is
arraigning those who have committed these crimes while still
offering external sacrifices (verses 16-21). Though God is
judge, God is also gracious in mercy. There is hope for those
who have a listening heart and turn from mere external offerings to offerings of praise and thanksgiving; these are true Jewish signs of a reconciliation on the part of the people. The last
verse of the psalm shows how gracious God is: "Honor to me is
a sacrifice of thanksgiving, to the upright I will show God's salvation" (NJB, Psalm 50:23).

Psalm 51

The Miserere is an individual lamentation
and one of the seven penitential psalms. This
psalm is a masterpiece for understanding the
depth of a person who is contrite and filled
with compunction. The transparency of this
person's crushed heart reaches out to the
mercy of God in such an honest confession of
sin that both in the synagogue and the church
this psalm touches the hearts of those praying it. I, too, have been
very moved by this psalm more than the other individual lamentations and have seen others sobbing after praying it.

The scholars do not agree regarding the origin proposed
by the inscription attached to the heading of the psalm, namely
that it was said after David realized his serious sins of adultery
and murder (2 Samuel 12). In reflecting on the Hebrew tradition of ascribing it to David, I realized that in the whole of the

Bible this application was very similar to what a passionate and contrite David could have expressed. So I remained with the inscription and read the psalm in the light of David's life involving his adulterous relationship with Bathsheba and his deliberate murder of Uriah, her husband. It is true that the psalm does conclude with verses offering a different perspective that fits the time of return to the ruins of Jerusalem and prior to the building of the second Temple. These lines seem to have been added to make the psalm a collective or national lamentation of one that was formerly so personal. The Soncino commentary maintains the Davidic origin: "Originally the psalm was a personal *cri du coeur* — so why not David's? — which was appropriately adopted for recital in a time of national humiliation; and then the prayer for the Temple's restoration was appended" (Cohen, 161).

One of the key words in the psalm is the word "heart." I have chosen the title "With a Listening Heart" for these reflections and certainly in this psalm the heart of the poet is totally transparent before God. It reaches out to the heart of God who is all mercy and love. The words "heart and spirit" are at the center of the outcry of the penitent and his need for God's forgiveness. Verse 10 is the key to the prayer and is divinely inspired: "Create in me a clean heart and put a new and steadfast spirit within me." The word used for "create" is the same word that God uses for the creation of the universe. This is quite dramatic then in asking that God fashion a totally new heart for this sinner so that he may interface with the mercy and compassion of God (verse 2); with the holy righteousness of God as his judge (verses 6 and 16); with the wisdom God gives (verse 8), and finally with salvation (verse 16).

Psalm 52

🦂

The Hebrew tradition frequently associates a psalm with an incident or historical event in the life of King David, the traditional author of the Book of Psalms. The psalms are referred back to 1 and 2 Samuel whenever there are such connecting events or situations for David. Did he then compose and sing a song? Scholars often reject such implications and associations, but frequently upon reading narratives about David one easily sees that the Jewish tradition makes sense. In this psalm the tradition associates Doeg, an official in Saul's court, as the evil culprit who is harassing David and spying on him. Though Doeg does not seem to be a slanderer, he is a betrayer and a murderer. By reading the life of David we help ourselves in understanding the psalms which are attributed to him through the captions called inscriptions written at the top of each psalm. This at least gives us a picture of what the psalms mean by "enemies," "oppressors," and "evil ones." The Soncino commentary on the psalms tells us, "It was certainly true of Doeg that his tongue brought destruction upon many" (Cohen, 52). He is the type of person described in this psalm even though the psalm may have been speaking of someone else at a different time in history.

The heart of this lamentation and its purpose is found in the opening verses 3-5. Here we see a champion or powerful man boasting of his wrongdoing and deeds of evil. God's power alone can silence him and bring him down. The psalmist is on his part convinced that "God's mercy endureth forever" (verse 3). This is what overcomes the braggart and "champion." A nonviolent Levite or servant of God prays and through God's justice and righteousness overcomes this evil warrior (verses 5-9). Psalm 1, which is a sapiential psalm, is easily related to this part of Psalm 52 in which the Levite compares himself to a leafy and healthy olive tree near God's Temple. We are in the area of the good versus the bad in our psalm. As our psalm comes to a conclusion, there is an expression or offering of thanksgiving demonstrating that one's prayer is answered: "I will give Thee thanks forever; because Thou hast done it" (verse 11).

Psalm 53

A wisdom psalm with much of Psalm 14 within it. Many commentators skip over this psalm and simply say it is a later emendation of Psalm 14. This is true for many of the verses, but it is different and has a right to be considered in itself as part of the canonical and inspired Book of Psalms. There had to be a deliberate decision about its being placed here by the compilers of the psalms, and the differences are important in studying each psalm as an inspired poem or song. First, its inscription is different; it is called a *maskil* or instruction which is sung in the Temple. It is also found in the second book of the psalms which are called Elohistic psalms contrasting them with those which are Yahwistic. This is seen in verse 3 where *Elohim* is translated as "God." There is also a difference in the more numerous enemies which are presented. Again in verse 5 *Elohim* is the name given for "God," whereas Psalm 14 uses *YHVH* or "Lord." In verse 6 the added expression, "where there was no fear," strengthens the contrast being made between the righteous and the evil ones. Verse 6 also adds, "Thou hast put them to shame, because God has rejected them." Again, the description of the evil ones is extended by the mention that God (*Elohim*) is carrying out his judgments upon them through rejecting them. Finally in verse 7 all is the same as in Psalm 14 except the use of *Elohim* instead of *YHVH*.

I found this helpful note in the Soncino commentary: "God (Elohim)... Lord (Yahweh but pronounced as Adonai). The traditional interpretation of the two divine names is God in His aspect of justice and mercy respectively" (Cohen, 179).

Our present psalm has a universal tone about it in comparison with Psalm 14 which seems to focus only on the people of Israel. Perhaps, we can see that we, too, in our recitation of familiar vocal prayers emphasize or even add some of our own words to express our feelings and pause to think about what we are saying while thinking with new expressions.

Psalm
54
♀

This psalm is a perfectly structured individual lamentation. A lamentation begins with the psalmist addressing God with a polite imperative form of a verb while also providing the motivation of the prayer and intercessory outcry. Then a reason or statement is given to explain what the circumstances for lamentation are for the individual. As the body or remainder of the psalm comes to a conclusion, a thanksgiving prayer, a promise, or an offering is expressed in the psalm. This demonstrates that God has already heard the prayer and was faithful to the promise of the covenant. These elements are easily seen in the psalm under consideration.

Though this is an individual or "I" psalm, it is easily adapted to a collective group worshiping in the Temple. Mowinckel tells us, "A great many (of the "I" psalms) are actually collective psalms in which an individual is speaking on behalf of the congregation. Psalm 54 is one of these" (1:217).

Weiser complains about the limits of this psalm by saying it is too subjective and anthropomorphic. However, in my own experience of praying, I sometimes pray for my personal concerns and intentions and for impossible situations, hoping against hope, that God will grant them. Our human prayers may seem very simple and even childish, but we are nevertheless communicating with our God through them, realizing we are like children begging for a present from a parent. I believe God hears these prayers, too, in many unsuspected ways. We realize sometime later that God has actually answered our prayers.

Psalm 55 ☙

This is classified as an individual lamentation. Yet, many scholars are in disagreement on its genre or type, its content, and the time of its writing — as is the case with many of our psalms. Despite the gaps that seem to be in this poem, it does turn out to be a psalm in which an I–Thou relationship has been broken. It also turns to other persons who seem to be oppressing the one who prays. In my estimation, in praying this psalm it is best to accept it as a unified piece of lamentation offered by a very troubled and distressed person who prays as best as he or she is able in these perplexing and overwhelming circumstances. Do we not often pray in such rambling, disjointed, and emotional ways whenever we are stressed out or whenever we have been betrayed by a dear friend? We experience sorrow and distress. The psalm, like our own prayer, is filled with sincere crying out to God who alone seems to be our friend. Only God is able to bring us through.

We see the background for the betraying friend in what is said in verses 12-15. But we also have, like the psalmist, many other enemies now, as described in the first part of the psalm. What is most upsetting is that these former friends and also our enemies are among our own and are not those attacking us from without our city, home or nation. With such conflicting and complicated situations, it is good for us to read the verses of the psalm which demonstrate confidence and trust in God. This will help us in our reflection and meditation on this psalm and we, too, will fly away like a dove to a deserted place or retreat so that we can pause and then take on life again. We leave aside the negative verses and the curses of our betrayer or enemies, and during the morning, afternoon, and evening turn to God alone (verse 17). Thus we are praying through our ordeal while saying with the psalmist, "I call upon God, and the Lord will save me!" (verse 16). We say, "Cast your burden on the Lord, and he will sustain you" (verse 22). And, "I will trust in you" (verse 23). We will find that our solution through prayer is not so different from that of the psalmist.

*Psalm
56*

🍃

This psalm was the prayer and individual lamentation of a person before the Exile (587 B.C.E.), but it has since been adapted to the people as a national lamentation. Mitchell Dahood considers it to be a lamentation of a king praying to God to be delivered from his slanderers. Thus the psalm seems to contain both the individual as well as the collective dimensions of a lamentation. In itself the psalm is one of a person of great faith and confidence in God. In the Soncino commentary it is called "the gem of quiet faith" (Cohen, 56). In its structure there is clear evidence of its having the components of a lamentation psalm: First, the introduction invokes God and gives a motivation; then, there is an expression of confidence which will be repeated as a refrain in the psalm; thirdly, there is a statement of the cause for the lamentation. Part two of the psalm, verses 8-10, is a prayer demonstrating once again the great faith and confidence of the psalmist. Finally, there is a closing with promise fulfilled and a thanksgiving hymn.

The beauty and the simplicity of this psalm lie in its offering to us expressions of hope, confidence and absolute trust in God. God will surely come to our aid; there is no doubt about this. We see that the psalmist is very much aware of the presence of God as he uses the title *Elohim* nine times; Lord or *YHVH* once; and a unique expression of God as the "Exalted One" (seen likewise in Psalm 7:8). This sets up a formidable contrast of God over against the oppressors who are "flesh," "mortal," and simply "human." These three different Hebrew words are used to show how weak the opposition is compared to Who God is.

This psalm strengthens us in the virtue of hope and trust in our relationship with God. The simplicity and absolute trust and confidence persist throughout the psalm and help us to do the same in our personal prayer.

Psalm 57

This is a sister psalm to the preceding one (Psalm 56). In this poem God is praised and exalted; the psalmist shows his unconditional trust in the Lord God because of the mercy and compassion and truth lavished upon him. The psalm is an individual lamentation in which we see a continuing theme of concern about the oppressors who slander and speak lies about the innocent, and possibly about our psalmist.

Weiser succinctly and clearly sums up this thread which appears so frequently in lamentation psalms: "Significantly, it is the offensive *word* which is continually stigmatized in the psalms as the most dangerous weapon in human conflict [cf. Pss. 12:2; 52:2; 55:3; 59:7; 64:3]" (427).

The psalm has the same structure as Psalm 56 in which the elements of an individual lamentation are clearly seen: In verses 1-6 we see the lamentation; in verses 7-11, the thanksgiving. There is also a *ritornello* in verses 6 and 12 which enhances the effectiveness of the sung prayer and continues to exude great confidence in God. "Be Thou exalted, O God, above the heavens; Thy glory be above all the earth."

In verses 8-11 we have some evidence that the psalms were sung to the accompaniment of musical instruments and thus the prayer is intensified and, so to speak, in singing them, we pray twice! We can in verse 8 visualize the psalmist awakening to the morning and breaking out in a joyful melody upon the harp and psaltery. A variety of instruments are mentioned in the psalms, for example, in our psalm the harp (*kinnor*) and the psaltery (*nevel*); in others the timbrel (*tof*), the trumpet (*shofar*), the pipe (*'ugab*), stringed instruments (*minim*), cymbals (*zelzelim*) and drums. Add to these instruments the beauty and power of the human voice and the clapping of hands. The psalm reads in verse 9, "Awake, my glory, awake psaltery and harp; I will awake the dawn." The Soncino commentary adds, "The Talmud quotes the phrase in support of the beautiful tradition that a harp hung above David's couch, and when the North wind touched its strings at midnight, producing sweet music, he arose to occupy himself with the study of the Torah" (Cohen, 182).

I also found the contrast in imagery imaginative and strong; oppressors are seen as lurking and roaring lions, while the psalmist or David is like a bird under the protective wings of God; nothing is to be feared. We do well in our personal prayer to sing and to overcome the troubles and negative feelings we have by focusing on the positive verses of praising God and having great confidence in God's presence and protection. These verses in our psalm outnumber the negative ones about oppressors.

Psalm 58

🎕

This psalm is similar in its expression to chapter 27 of Deuteronomy where a discourse on blessings and curses from the twelve tribes is given and measured out from the twin peaks of Mount Gerizim and Ebal in Samaria. The tribes are divided equally and one set gives the blessings from one mount, while the other six tribes do it from Mount Ebal. In our Psalm 58 we may have a priest or Levite who sounds very much like a prophet in his excoriation of the wickedness and evil that he is experiencing from the leaders and judges of his own nation. This is always a dreadful situation for a people, and complaints or lamentations are in order.

The imagery of the psalm is quite graphic and striking as the unjust judges are compared to snakes, asps, lions and even to a snail! (The only reference to a snail in all of the Bible.) This psalm shows evidence of being an ancient one; its vocabulary is difficult and there are some gaps. Some of the vengeful dimensions of the psalmist are shocking for our "pious ears." How are we able to pray such a psalm?

I think we are able to reach a solution to the curse psalms and others that are vindictive by reflection and patience with the strong language and the imprecations against the wicked. In looking at the opening verses of the psalm we see that it is bad leadership from the judges and rulers that disturbs the person who composed this psalm. He poses a question and then only in the conclusion of the psalm do we have an answer that soothes our thirst for prayer in this psalm. God is the judge who rewards the righteous and will take care of the evildoers. "This psalmist's fiery indignation against unjust judges and evildoers generally is not kindled by personal wrongs. The psalm comes hot from a heart lacerated by the sight of widespread corruption" (Cohen, 183). The psalm concludes in this beautiful answer to the query posed at the beginning: "Then men will say, 'Surely, the righteous has fruit; yea, there is still a God who sees that justice is done on earth.'" Amen.

Psalm 59

This psalm is considered both an individual lamentation and a public lamentation. It has characteristics within it that make it proper for a king to be leading the congregation that has gathered for worship of God as king at the covenant festival in pre-exilic times. If considered as an individual lament the Hebrew tradition sets it during the time Saul was pursuing David and his men as narrated in 1 Samuel 22. We have seen this tradition applied to other psalms in the second collection of psalms. Our psalm would then be in a sequence similar to the Psalm 58.

This psalm is a fine work of structural and literary composition. In the first five lines we are in contact with the principal ideas of the psalmist's or David's prayer. Present in this psalm are two refrains or responses that separate the lamentation mode from the second part which is more a thanksgiving psalm. The refrains are found in verses 6 and 14, and in 9 and 17.

The names used for God in the psalm are both *YHVH Sabaoth*, the preferred name for God in Temple worship, and *Elohim*, the name showing God in relationship to all nations. The congregation and the psalmist praying in the Temple await a manifestation of God's presence near or over the ark of the covenant. God is presented as a high tower, a refuge, a strength, and a fortress. These images do suggest the king having a role in the leading of this song while the congregation listens or responds in choirs. In our own praying of this psalm, we do well to recognize these names and attributes of God. This will aid our meditation or recitation of the psalm and others like it that have phrases which disturb us by their violent language or vengeful spirit. I suggest that we think of God as delivering us from all sorts of evil, sin, and oppression. Let these and sin be our enemies as we pray with the psalmist. Verse 17 is a good refrain: "O my strength, I will sing praises to Thee, for God is my fortress, the God of my mercy." Deliverance from all sorts of evils and "enemies" is reassured for those who recite and sing this psalm.

Psalm 60
༅

This psalm is classified as a public lamentation which deals with the nation's defeat in a recent battle. The poet wrestles with the question, "God, why have you done this to us, your beloved people?" In order to understand many of the geographical references and battles, it is worthwhile to read 2 Samuel 8 which is a summary of David's campaigns against the neighboring warlords. Keep in mind, we are not able to place the psalm within the exact historical context as is the case with many psalms. Moreover, the superscriptions in the

Hebrew tradition are not always consonant with what the scholars suggest as the occasion for a given psalm; but, as pointed out,
these musical settings do give us a possible background for the
psalm. Certainly this psalm is filled with military symbolism
and language and parts of it could actually go back to pre-exilic
times and even to the time of David.

Such psalms may be difficult to pray, but upon further
reflection they are definitely a form of inspired prayer for the
communities that use the psalms, both Jewish and Christian.
It is helpful to look at the deeper religious dimension within
each psalm. As Sigmund Mowinckel points out, "Prayer to the
'God of revenge' must be taken to express the knowledge and
the faith that God will not allow justice to be violated" (Mowinckel, 1:204).

In this psalm we see many modes and moods of prayer.
Lamentation, prayer of intercession and invocation, an oracle,
and a *anamnesis* or a remembering of how God acts in salvation
history (*Heilsgeschichte*), and finally a trust or confidence in
God's promise in the last verse.

In the back pages of many Bibles there are maps which indicate the location of the place names and territories given in
the psalms. It is helpful to locate them and to recognize the tribal
locations. Those that belong to Israel at this time are Shechem,
Gilead, Manasseh, Ephraim, and Judah; the enemy territories
are Edom, Moab, Philistia and northern Syria. Geography plays
a vital part in the salvation history of the Bible and also in its
theology.

Some parts of this psalm are repeated elsewhere in the
Psalter. We have already noticed this with Psalms 14 and 53.
Here verses 5-12 are recorded in Psalm 108:6-12. Psalm 44 is
also helpful for understanding the tone and situation in our
psalm. It gives us a similar perspective for a nation in time of a
defeat. I found that Weiser gives us a great insight into the

deeper religious dimension when he comments, "The actual affliction about which they here complain is the spiritual affliction of a nation who knows itself to be rejected by God in his anger and yet are neither able nor willing to let him go. However, the fact that this shock to their faith does not lead them to doubt about God or to rebellion against him, but is expressed in prayer to him, shows how deeply rooted that faith in God is and how serious the people's attitude to God as they pray. It is only when spiritual affliction reaches these utmost depths that it is capable of becoming the only means of overcoming every adversity" (Weiser, 439).

Psalm 61

An individual lamentation with a prayer for the welfare of the king. Scholars are divided on the type of psalm this is, despite its being only nine verses long. They are equally divided on the social location of the psalm and on its historical determination. We know that the psalms extend from the time of David (1000 B.C.E.) to the Maccabean period (163 to 63 B.C.E.); frequently scholars will range in dating a psalm from one end of this time frame to the other. Whenever this occurs, it is best to take their agreement on the structure and versification and to follow the Hebrew tradition for background information on the spirit of the psalm. Thus commentators are in agreement on the opening of the psalm having a double invocation, a prayer, and a statement or cause for the lament or petition (verses 2-3). Verses 4-6 are a strong expression of confidence in God. Verses 7-8 are a prayer for the welfare of the king. Verse 9 is a final promise that is fulfilled. The Hebrew tradition fixes this psalm in the time that David was in exile from the holy city of Jerusalem because of the rebellious Absalom, his son. This story is presented in 2 Samuel 15:13-18 and fits the mood and situation described in our psalm.

The psalmist or the king desires to be in the sacred prayer place of Jerusalem near the ark of the covenant. In our own experience there are sacred places where we find respite from stress and our daily chores and responsibilities. This may be a chapel, a synagogue, a mosque, a shrine, or a retreat center. Just as this was a desire of the psalmist, it, too, is a desire for us to be in such a place when we feel a lot of pressure. We then pray and thank God for such an opportunity. Verse 5, in my estimation, is the key to the heart of this psalm: "I will dwell in Thy tent forever; I will take refuge in the covert of Thy wings."

Psalm 62

In this psalm of confidence, the psalmist sees and experiences that God alone is his refuge. The expression, "God alone," in six verses shows us the emphatic style of the song when it describes trust in God. Only a number of psalms are classified as psalms of confidence (Pss. 3, 11, 16, 23, 27:1-6, 41, 62, 131). They are usually placed under the larger category of individual laments, but their thrust is predominantly that of absolute trust in God. The opening verse of the psalm is found in verse 2 and this is the key to the message: "My soul in stillness waits, for in God alone is my salvation." This is repeated as an inclusion and/or refrain in verse 5 thus encasing the "case" or reason why the person is praying this psalm. God is a "rock, a fortress or tower, and a strength" for the poet. I see verses 6-8 and parallels which further explain this confidence in God and lead the singer to invite the people to have the same devotion and disposition as his. He also is concerned that he not be brought down to the class of evildoers, who are inferred in verses 4 and 5 and whose crimes are stealing, lying, and tearing down of people.

This psalm is focused in such a way that it helps us remember to start our prayers in the presence of God and to continue them in that presence. It is true that God alone can redeem us and prevent us from succumbing to evil desires or deeds. We are to be alone with God. We can imagine the psalmist praying before the ark of the covenant in the Temple while inviting those standing near to participate in his prayer. His heart is lifted up to the God of mercy and who will render to everyone according to their works (verse 13). I find this psalm to be consoling and encouraging.

Psalm 63
꧂

This individual lament displays an extraordinary longing and yearning to be in the presence of God in the sanctuary in Jerusalem near the ark of the covenant. The traditional perspective puts this psalm during the time of David's sojourn in the wilderness while fleeing from his rebellious son Absalom who wishes to take over the kingdom. His meditation (or that of the psalmist) brings him to reflect and ponder how good it would be to have an intimate communion with God in Jerusalem. There God's mercy and justice are experienced and one's prayer is answered. Oh, that this could be now! The person meditating continues to do so throughout the three watches of the night according to the division of the night at that time in Israel (verse 7). God means everything to him and he blesses God as long as he is alive. He lifts his hands, as do the Levites in the Temple, up to God as a symbol of offering his heart to God (verses 5-9). He likens his soul to the dry, parched land surrounding him. He thirsts for God's presence as land thirsts for water. The richness of the offerings in Jerusalem are remembered and he yearns all the more to be there. While praying thus, he uses the phrase, "My soul cleaves to you." This is the same verb used for the embrace of love between passionate spouses (*davaq*). Among the Jewish mystics this term came to represent their sense of devotion, rapt attachment, a person's absorption in relationship to God, especially in prayer (Cohen, 198). Thus our psalm touches the depth of Israelite piety and devotion to God through prayer.

I recite this psalm quite often and it has been one of my favorites for years. It expresses an I-Thou relationship with God and combines contemplation with love of God. I am thankful for the person who composed this poem whether it be David, a minister of the Jerusalem Temple, or one of the composers of songs for the Temple.

Psalm 64

This is an individual lament with a theme of trust in God. The psalmist has a gift for clever play on words in the original Hebrew text and gives us a very dramatic and great reversal seen in the conflict situation with the evildoers or scandalmongers. The psalm has all of the characteristics of the structure of a lamentation: verses 2 and 3 invoke God directly with an imperative, "Hear! Save!"; then presents his conflict "case" or reason for the lament in verses 4-7. The castigation of the evil men is seen in verse 8 and 9. Through the use of a word that could also be read as "see" rather than "fear," verse 10 could be changed to: "All will see and declare the work of God and understand his doing." This is part of the clever way in which the poet uses the word for "see" and "fear" throughout several verses, for the words in Hebrew are similar. The author favors another word which leads from the first part of his psalm to the second, namely, the word "suddenly" (*pitom*).

As in other lamentation psalms the oppressors wound and kill with their tongues. This is the dreaded weapon they use with venomous and destructive words used like poisoned arrows aimed at killing an innocent person. The great surprise for these malefactors is that God turns the tables on them and shoots his arrows of truth that are fatal. This is a great dramatic reversal in the psalm. I see these evil liars as those who do not have a listening heart. From the caverns of their hearts come evil designs and thoughts of harming the innocent. God's heart and the hearts of the just are so much more profound in goodness and righteousness compared to their oppressors' proclivity toward evil.

I relate this psalm to the power of fear which often cripples us from doing things. It frequently makes us immobile, anxious, and depressed. Praying this psalm can help us to be aware of fear and to overcome it along with human respect, realizing and trusting in God who overturns the false fears and useless worries that we suffer from time to time. The last verse refers to a heart that listens without fearing: "And all the upright in heart shall glory" (verse 11). As a postscript, this psalm is similar in structure and message to Psalm 37.

Psalm 65 ☙

A hymn of collective thanksgiving offered in the Temple. This song, filled with praise and thanksgiving, has three parts. The Hebrew tradition keeps the psalm unified. There is no way of knowing the exact time when it was written nor what event is intended. In the first part, verses 2 through 5, we experience a prayer of thanksgiving and praise; there is also a formula indicating the need for God's forgiveness within these verses. Thus in the introduction several primary attitudes of prayer are to be found in the song. All have a reverent and trustful disposition toward God who is present in the sanctuary of the Temple where the ark of the covenant rests. Part two praises God's awe-inspiring creation which is symbolized by the mountains and the waters of the seas. Joined to the roaring of the waves is the tumult of the peoples who are also God's creation. Thus the creation of God is seen as God's work and it, too, is to be praised in the sanctuary of the Temple. Verses 5 to 8 make up this second part of the psalm. The third part is indicative of a celebration for the harvest; probably this is the great pilgrimage feast of *Sukkot* or Tabernacles occurring in the fall. God is seen like the great caretaker of the fields of grain and the meadows and, as God rides a chariot, the rain clouds douse the land and make its furrows fertile. Thus God, nature, and humans are all part of the content of this hymn. We will see similar thanksgiving hymns celebrated by the community of Israel in Psalms 66, 67, 68, 118, and 124.

This psalm makes us aware of the various ways and modes of prayer in which we are able to thank and praise God. Nature speaks to us of God's presence in the way fruitful trees and golden meadows display God's beneficence. Then Zion is seen as the home for the sanctuary which is a sacred place for the presence of God. I find myself summing up my sentiments and devotion in verse five: "Happy the one whom Thou chosest, and bringest near, to dwell in Thy courts."

Psalm
66
❧

This psalm is a hymn of thanksgiving for deliverance; it is both a hymn of the community as well as an individual hymn as is evident in verses 13-20. The psalm starts with a jubilant shout to God from all the earth. God's name and glory are praised. This high-spirited introduction leads the congregation into admiring the great marvels God has done for the people by liberating them from Egypt. Thus the great event of the Exodus is recalled as well as the crossing over the river Jordan into the Promised Land. The nations are called upon to recognize these mighty acts of God.

Verses 8 through 12 continue the community thanksgiving while recalling the difficulties and sufferings that Israel experienced before coming to the aforementioned deliverance. Then the individual singer or psalmist voices either in his own person or perhaps the king himself leads the people gathered in the Temple to fulfill the vows that attest to God's having acted on behalf of God's people. His burnt offering attests that God did this and will continue to do this. Fulfillment is implied when vows are made in the Temple. The past events become alive in the celebration of song and sacrifices offered.

This psalm closely resembles the majestic and victorious song of Moses or Miriam as presented in Exodus 15:4-10, 16-18. The ritual, worship, and singing make that song come alive once again as the king and choirs alternate. Neither God's attentiveness nor his mercy are lacking in what is now happening and what happened then.

This made me recall my own celebration in a home of some Jewish friends from a Hebrew class in Jerusalem (Ulpan Etz Zion) where the participants actually narrate the Exodus and take themselves there to be present in the crossing of the Red Sea and in entering the Promised Land. This story is filled with freedom and joy and the children participate by asking certain leading questions that make this night so different from all other nights. The entire family is a part of the story and the reality. Just as in this psalm, all praise God. As a non-Jew, I too was able to join in and celebrate this sacred liberation of God's people. I sensed the foundation pillars of their and my liberation through faith in the One God of mercy and fidelity.

Psalm 67

This, too, is a community thanksgiving psalm. The opening is a paraphrase of the most beautiful prayer called the Aaronic blessing or the priestly prayer found in Numbers 6:24f. "The Lord bless you and keep you! The Lord let his face shine upon you, and be gracious to you! The Lord look upon you kindly and give you peace!" Most commentaries place this psalm in the setting of the celebration of the feast of Tabernacles, an autumn feast of the harvest. I like the new insight of M. Lazarus who argues for a nonliteral interpretation of verse seven. Then the verse would refer to the "produce" not of the fields but of God's overseeing of everything on the earth through God's moral rule and ever-watchful eye. This is more consonant with the lofty spiritual tone of the psalm. Lazarus states "that all nations praise God, for his moral government of the world is the highest 'product' of the whole of life on earth" (cited in Cohen, 208).

I thoroughly enjoyed reflecting and praying this psalm because it has no trace of anxiety, fear, or oppression from enemies. After a string of individual lamentations, this psalm refreshes the thirsty soul. Its joyful praises are a fitting way to honor God the Creator with a human heart filled with thanksgiving for the God of all good gifts from above.

Psalm 68

This is one of the most remarkable psalms in the Psalter. It is classified as a thanksgiving hymn of the community of Israel. If anyone needs to know what salvation history entails, it can be experienced in reading this psalm. Despite the problems within the text itself because of gaps and guesswork on the part of those who handed it down, we have a splendid panorama of God's victories splashed before us on the canvas of Israel's *Heilsgeschichte*. Though the psalm can be considered to have several different songs within it, I prefer to stay with those exegetes who keep it intact. This does not prevent us from appreciating the wide strokes of artistry achieved by our poet.

One amazing discovery for me was the numerous names used for God. This is unique to the psalm and it surpasses any other part of the Bible in such a multiplicity of divine namings like: *Elohim, Yah, Adonai, Shaddai, YHVH, El, YHVH-Adonai, Elohim-Adonai, Melekh,* in verse 5, "The Rider of the Clouds," and in verse 9, "The One of Sinai." This may be an indication of how God was invoked by the Israelites at various stages of their salvation history.

The sources for this psalm are two of the most ancient

hymns or songs in the Bible, namely, the Song of Deborah in Judges 5 and that of Moses-Miriam in Exodus 15 where much of the imagery is repeated in our psalm.

The chronological extent and geographic sweep of the psalm may cover one thousand years of history and locations from Mount Hermon in Syria all the way to the land of Ethiopia in Africa! All throughout the psalm the tone and atmosphere is jubilant and triumphant for it is celebrating the victories of God and God's people Israel. It seems to call for a time when both kingdoms of the north and south were united. I conjecture the reign of Solomon for its setting.

Other parts of the *Tanakh* (Hebrew Bible) are remembered in reciting the psalm: Exodus, Numbers, Deuteronomy, Joshua, Judges, 1 Samuel, Isaiah, and some psalms. The poet knew his Bible! We have a procession similar to the dancing of Miriam and David who danced before the ark as this festive song is sung in approaching the Temple in Zion, the Holy City of Jerusalem. There we may see the tribes of Benjamin, Zebulun, Judah, and Napthali moving up the stairs to the inner walls of the Temple (see verse 21). There both the giving of the covenant and the freeing of the people of Israel are celebrated. This whole sung story is totally God-centered in the splendid liturgy and ritual of the Temple priests, Levites and singers. All of God's victories are being recalled and relived in the sacred presence of God near the ark of the covenant. "The psalm stands as a monument of the invincible faith and inextinguishable hopes of Israel, and a prophecy of spiritual glories in part realized, in part yet to come" (Cohen, 68).

In praying and reflecting upon the colorful imagery and its God-centeredness in all of the victories, I was thrilled and exhilarated by the tremendously vast sweep of events and the jubilant expressions used within this prayer. I hesitated writing about it for it covers almost the whole Bible and yet is a unified sketch in broad strokes from the genius lyricist who composed it.

Psalm 69 ჻

This is considered as an individual lamentation psalm. We do not know who the author is nor when it was composed though there are similarities to the life of the prophet Jeremiah. Certain parts of it have been seen before in other lamentation psalms but there is a tendency to use some of the same images of oppression from the enemy. I nevertheless like to look at it as a unified piece and I include the final verses as well even though many commentators would ascribe them to a different writer and a different epoch. Mitchell Dahood places the psalm during the time of Exile in Babylon; others take it down to the time of the Maccabees. It is a psalm that has been a favorite for citations in the New Testament and in the early Christian writers where it takes on a messianic perspective. I do not think it was considered messianic in the Hebrew tradition. Since I am more concerned with staying within the boundaries of the text itself as presented in the Hebrew, I refrain from reading Christological ideas or meanings into it. The psalm speaks for itself within the tradition in which it was written.

As in all lamentations, the psalm begins by invoking God and then offering a complaint! Then a specific reason is given for the complaint and this is usually followed by a prayer. The psalmist uses the powerful imagery of great bodies of water threatening to drown him so he calls out for help from God who alone can be a safe and sheltering rock for him. God alone can deliver him from the accusations and evils heaped upon his head like a waterfall by members of his own family and nation. His personal pain is felt within the song. Even at the city gates where the sages gathered to discuss things, our psalmist is made sport of and is included in the songs loved by drunks! They taunt him with making him pay for what he has not stolen. Nevertheless, the God-oriented prayers break through in the psalm for he confesses his own guilt and waits patiently for God's intervention. He hopes. Then in verse 10 we see the passion and zeal of the psalmist showing the "fire that he has in his belly": "Because zeal for Thy house has eaten me up, and the reproaches of them that reproach Thee are fallen upon me." He as a devout and zealous man weeps, prays, and fasts. In verses 14 and 17 we are at the core of his prayer as he calls upon the mercy (*ḥesed*) and the abundant compassion (*reḥem*) and truth of God's salvation (*emet*). Thus God is good and compassionate in an overwhelming way.

In the second half of the psalm, the poet wants God to turn the tables on his enemies — those who mock, taunt, and criticize him and possibly even condemn him to prison for stealing. His outcries are like curses heaped upon their heads. We may find this difficult for our own prayer, but can't we understand such passion and vehement language from a devout zealot who is pushed against the wall? Probably not! But God understands such language, and the poet is confident that God will prevail. Only God could and does really understand us when we are angry and do not know what to say in our prayers.

In the end, the psalm does include a thanksgiving hymn because God always hears the cry of the poor (verse 34). Our psalmist hopes for the salvation of Zion and the rebuilding of the cities of Judah. Finally, I add one last thought from the Soncino commentary: "This psalm should be read throughout with Jeremiah in mind; whether he wrote it or not, his history gives the key to its meaning" (Cohen, 216).

Psalm 70
♱

This individual lament is a reproduction of Psalm 40:14-18 with a number of textual variants, for example, God's name is *Elohim* whereas in Psalm 40 it is *YHVH*. The psalm is a clear cry for help from God who is invoked in a Temple liturgy. It has similar ideas as Psalm 69 in words and theme. The introductory verse has a certain urgency in its plea for help. The opening is similar to the closing of the psalm and thus forms an inclusion with it.

Often such direct and simple prayer to God is just what we need. It is like a javelin thrown into the heavens to catch God's attention. We need help right away. We, like the psalmist are among the *'anavim,* the poor of God who depend totally on God. No one else is able to help. We end with the psalm's plea, "O Lord, tarry not!" (verse 6). "The gleam of confidence is changed to a call of need, and the tone of the whole psalm is thereby made more plaintive" (Cohen, 222).

Psalm 71
♱

This is an individual psalm of lamentation which has a strong theme of confidence in God within its verses. It issues from the lips of an elderly person, probably a Levite who is devout and immersed in the tradition of the other psalms. He seems to be aware that his days are numbered. This poet is a tried and true traditionalist who remembers and repeats many of the cultic psalms in his own composition. It results in a magnificent personal summary of his life, almost a psalmist's journal or diary. He is not merely repeating what he has heard sung in the Temple, he is reliving it. They are part of his daily way of praying. In looking at the verses we will find that he is borrowing phrases and themes from at least fifteen other psalms. Among his favorites are Psalms 31, 35, and 40.

He demonstrates his absolute trust in God's protection from his birth (verse 6), through his youth (verses 5, 17), into his present aging condition (verses 9 and 18). We are entering into his own pondering on the meaning of his life as expressed in his lamentation, his praise, and his thanksgiving. For him, with God, "life is worth living."

His image of God is a strong one of God as a powerful protector. He describes God as his sheltering rock, his fortress, strength, and his refuge. God is his hope, his justice and holiness, and his trust as he shouts out, "O God, who is like unto Thee?" (verse 19). The Levite calls God the Holy One of Israel, a title only found in Psalms 78:41 and 89:19. The Soncino commentary has this to say about the title "Holy One of Israel": "Commonly used of God in Isaiah, but in the Psalter only lxxviii. 41, lxxxix, 19. It denotes that God in His character of a Holy God has entered into covenant with Israel, and His holiness is pledged to redeem His people" (Cohen, 226).

As a septuagenarian I find this psalm consoling. I am led through similar sentiments as I read and ponder over its verses and as I think of the years that have gone by. I remember some of my favorite scriptural passages and vocal prayers. Yes, this psalm is a handy compendium for psalms that have an individual and personal tone. Finally, this psalm has an introduction taken from Psalm 31. It goes from invoking God, to prayer, acts of confidence in God, lamentation, trust and then a hymn of thanksgiving with a promise to continue as a faithful Levite. This is an excellent prayer for growing old gracefully.

Psalm 72

This is one of the few royal psalms along with Psalms 2, 18, 20, 21, 45, 72, 89, 101, 110, 132, 144. Our psalm is considered to be messianic within the later Jewish tradition in the Talmud; in Christian theology it is considered messianic even though this psalm is not cited in the New Testament. Today's exegesis tends to disagree with the messianic interpretation.

This psalm was used in the Temple either at the beginning of the New Year or at the enthronement of *YHVH* and the coronation of a king of Judah. The psalm initially describes the king's ethical responsibilities for the poor and the widows; then follow the prayers wishing the king a long and blessed reign (verses 5-7; 8-14), and blessings and prayers for prosperity in the kingdom (verses 15-17). The most extended doxology in the Psalter then concludes the psalm with a reference to David as the one responsible for some of the psalms in the Elohist collection (Psalms 42-72).

It is not possible to identify the historical period nor the king through the psalm. The superinscription attributes it to Solomon but that is a scribal addition. For our personal meditation, it is helpful to imagine the king to be Solomon who enjoyed such a peaceful and extensive kingdom. One can imagine a Levite singing this psalm and offering the prayers for King Solomon on the occasion of his accession to the throne. The whole tone of the psalm is idealistic and idyllic.

The psalm is asking God to bless this king who in turn is to serve the poor and needy. It is they who join in the praise of God and the qualities of the king. His justice, mercy, and judgment are righteous. The praise is somewhat similar to that given to the idealized Hebrew woman in Proverbs 31:10-31 which is an acrostic composition (one using all the letters of the Hebrew

alphabet to express a thought about her). Great emphasis is put
on the king's attention to the needy, the humble, the poor, and
those who are desperate. The Hebrew text has a different word
for each of these groupings of the people.

The universality of the kingdom is idealized and set between the great river Euphrates and the other bodies of water
known by the poet. Finally, for our personal reflection, it is God
who is the king over Israel, and David and Solomon are God's
servants.

Psalm
73
℞

This psalm starts the third collection or book
of psalms according to the Hebrew superscription. The psalm is composed under the
name of Asaph who was the ancestor of the
temple musicians. There are 11 such Asaph
psalms (73-83), and Psalm 50 is likewise under his name. This is considered to be a wisdom or didactic psalm; a few scholars would
list it as a thanksgiving psalm because of its conclusion. Similar to the Book of Job, this psalm struggles with the question of
how can God permit evil and why bad things happen to good
people. It seems to be the personal reflection of a Levite, one
who serves and sings in the Temple, who is struggling with this
issue. There are some difficult passages in it because of the vocabulary and images as well as the state of the manuscript, but
as a unit it does stay with the theme in a coherent and clear presentation.

It can quickly be broken into several parts: Verses 1
through 3 are a statement of the psalmist in what is challeng-
ing his faith and disturbing his conscience. The arrogant,
healthy in body, and the slanderous are trying his confidence
in God. Verses 4-12 describe these proud-mouthed boasters of

evil. Verses 13-17 give us the inward struggle of the Levite and how he finally has a breakthrough in a religious experience during his prayer in the Temple. Verses 18-22 present what really will happen to these evildoers. Verses 23-28 are a final resolution and an act of thanksgiving and praise for the God who is good to those who are just. Though some speculate there may be a reference to an afterlife with God in this psalm, the majority agree that the benefits and blessings of God come to the Levite in this life. Most psalms do not treat of the afterlife with God. They deal with the practical religious concerns of people who are living in the time in which the psalm is sung. We need to wrestle with such a powerful psalm which despite not thinking of an afterlife with God does come to a godly solution that brings peace and confidence to the one who offered this piece of wisdom to us.

We are helped by praying the first line of the psalm and when we come to the last lines we realize we have bookends or an inclusion that is giving us the solution to the problem of theodicy raised in the body of the composition. Through the psalm we can easily follow the tortuous reflections of a Levite who is troubled by his experience of evil in the person of others who are arrogant, contemptuous of God, and slanderous of their neighbors. The trial of faith is resolved in such verses as verse 1, 7, 23, 25, 26, and 28. I like to combine verses 23 and 25 into the realm of a listening heart: "Nevertheless I am continually with Thee; Thou holdest my right hand. Whom have I in heaven but Thee? And beside Thee I desire none on earth."

Psalm

74

🙖

This is a national lamentation psalm. An individual may intone it in the Temple for the whole community. It is a good model for this class of psalms, since it has all the components of a lamentation within it. Other psalms having a similar pattern and belonging to the same genre are Psalms 12, 44, 58, 60, 77, 79, 80, 82, 83, 85, 90, 94, 106, 108, 123, 126 and 137.

Our psalm is similar in tone as well as in words to the Book of Lamentations, chapter two. The lamentation demonstrates the sadness and consternation the people of Israel feel about the destruction of their Temple in Jerusalem. They are most likely in exile in Babylon (modern Iraq) around the years between 527 and 522 B.C.E.

The psalm may be meditated upon in three distinct parts: verses 1-11 are a graphic description of the profanation of the Temple, its walls, its sanctuary; a plea or lament is offered to God to help the people understand why this has happened. The next section, verses 12-17 are a remembering of God's power in creation and in the Exodus event. This is definitely a history of salvation *anamnesis* or remembering. In verses 18-23 there is an ardent prayer and plea for help from the God who acts in history to a people who continue to believe and trust in God's power and fidelity. After all, Israel is God's flock, the family belonging to God, and Mount Zion is God's precious possession. Remembering is important in this psalm. On three occasions the word for "to remember" is used (*zakhar*): verses 2, 18, and 22.

I appreciated the feelings this psalm evokes in my own prayer and meditation. There is a gift in remembering the times when God helped me in some difficult situation or during a time of trial or illness. In a certain sense, each one of us participates in a cosmic salvation history (*Heilsgeschichte*), but we have our personal salvation histories as well. We, like the people in the psalm, remember the sacred events and places where we sensed the comfort of the presence of God. We learn from the remembering of Israel and we, too, have the foundation for hope. Coupled with our remembering is our crying out to God during difficult and trying times when it seems we are backed against the wall. We find God breaking through in creation as happens in this psalm in its central section. We learn how to pray with the people of God, Israel, while asking the question, why does this happen to us now? How long will it last? Will I be able to endure it? We learn that such lamentation is a true and appropriate form of prayer to a God who, though hidden, is also present to us in the paradox of our suffering and our hope.

Psalm 75

This psalm is classified by several as a psalm of *YHVH* (Lord) as king. It is complementary to Psalm 74. Mitchell Dahood has this informative sentence: "This brief poem, composed in archaic language that resembles the wording of the Song of Hannah (1 Samuel 2:1-10), contains twelve divine names — hence more titles and names than the number of verses — five of which have cropped up by applying the principles of northwest Semitic grammar and lexicography" (2:210). Dahood is speaking of Ugaritic, a language that has helped us understand the Hebrew text by studying the forerunner of many Hebrew words and phrases. For me, this is helpful for praying the psalms, for placing myself in the presence of God during prayer and addressing God with these appellatives: O God, Name, O Near One, Exalted One, Ancient Mountain,

Psalm 75

Victor (twice), God, *YHVH*, the Eternal, God of Jacob, and Just One. Incidentally, Islam has 99 attributes naming Allah!

The psalm contains a hymnal introduction sung in the Temple on the occasion of the feast of the kingship of *YHVH*. Then in verses three and four we have the oracle or actual words of God stating that God alone is the righteous judge and it is foolhardy for humans to be so arrogant as to defy this. The psalm then concludes with extolling and praising God who will break the horns of the wicked while being exalted as the Just One, that is, *YHVH* King of Israel.

The psalm has several symbols that make it quite colorful in expression and imagery. The word horn is used, referring to the horns of an animal, and signifies strength and power and even haughtiness. The cup filled with foaming and potent wine is a symbol for the fate and judgment of mortals. It is their lot in life. In this psalm the cup is indicative of the judgment passed on the arrogant. There is also the symbol of the pillars of the earth in verse 4 which shows God as the one who upholds all creation in the three-tiered concept of the ancients. The earth would be supported by these gigantic pillars above the waters. God, of course, in this psalm is the Creator, the protector and especially the judge over all things and persons.

In praying and reflecting on this psalm, I am able to sense the presence of God in the many ways in which the psalmist addresses or names God. I can attune myself to the oracular pronouncement given in the initial verses, after the invocation. The colorful symbols and images help me to understand how we humans are going to be judged by God who is king and judge over all of us and over creation.

Finally, there are other psalms in which God is centered upon as king which may help my understanding of this particular psalm. The following are such *YHVH* as king psalms: 47, 93, 96, 97, 98, and 99.

**Psalm
76**

🙢

This is a hymn dedicated to Zion, the holy city of Jerusalem. It is filled with the theme of salvation history, a celebration of the cult of the Temple honoring the kingship of God who is also a judge of all peoples and creatures. The psalm may also have an eschatological meaning in the last verses; that is, it looks toward the future of peace under God's protection.

The first four verses center on the celebration in the Temple while recalling the sacred history of Israel under David. It could even be a reminiscence of David conquering the citadel of Zion when he overcame the Jebusites. Zion then becomes a perfect symbol for Israel and still is today.

Verses 5 through 7 show God's mighty power and his action sends fear into all of Israel's enemies. Victories throughout the past testify to this and all are due to God's love for and protection of Israel. The psalm ends calling all to worship and to honor God by offering thanksgiving and praise.

This psalm made me think of the importance of authentic tradition. Tradition is seen in many ways in the psalms whenever God's marvelous acts are recounted and remembered. The variety of ways this is expressed helps us get a feel for a living tradition such as the Jews have always had. The past events are celebrated in many texts and in cult worship services both in the past when there was a Temple and today in the synagogues. The strands which have come down to us in the psalms demonstrate how these sacred acts of God saved the people then and do so now. Such a reverence for true tradition enables the people of today to live out in the present time the wonderful and marvelous deeds of *YHVH* or what classical language calls the *Magnalia Dei.*

Hope and confidence are thus kept alive in the community

of believers who pray that God will continue to do what God has enacted and accomplished in the past. We, in turn, are to remain faithful to our belief in God and to render thanks especially in sacred places where we have an opportunity to pray and think about these marvels of God. God always rules and judges us with righteousness and tender love when we are faithful to our belief in God as judge and king of our lives. There are living traditions in families, too, and in religions which center upon God as Creator and redeemer. I sensed this in my own tradition through reading and studying this psalm. I found that by reading Psalm 48 in relationship to the themes of this psalm, I had an even broader insight into the meaning of the present psalm.

Psalm 77
〄

This psalm was written during a time of exile (587-522 B.C.E.). It is classified as a public lamentation by most scholars. This is called the Babylonian captivity for the Jewish people. They yearned for a return to Judah and hoped for a rebuilding of Jerusalem. The psalmist in this prayer laments for the entire community of Israel. He may be a Levite and a former attendant for the Temple and its rituals. Now he spends the entire night in profound reflection on what has happened. He is troubled and is sorrowful. Verse 9 seems to capture his feelings and is the bottom line of his lamentation that is sung or chanted for the whole community. He is saying, "Will God's kindness and mercy towards us as a nation utterly cease, and his promises fail us forever?" As we read through this psalm we discover this poet meditates, ponders over, reflects upon, prays and laments over the seemingly divine abandonment. He shows us many modes of communicating with God throughout the psalm. These key words unite both parts of the psalm.

Part one consists of verses 2 through 13 and definitely has all of the characteristics of a lamentation. Part two, on the other hand, resembles a thanksgiving offered to God as the psalmist recalls the Exodus and God's great redemptive act in giving Israel its freedom from slavery in Egypt. Thus the people and the psalmist have some hope of future redemption while they are in exile. The remembering of this great miracle of God for Israel gives them hope for the future.

For both the psalmist and for us there is a form of prayer in which we ponder over and try to realize how God feels about us during a time in which we do not sense God's presence. Perhaps, this makes us realize that we often abandon all thought about God when we are successful or just too busy to think about God. However, when we return to this form of prayer we are in communication with God and we then realize that God gives us strength to endure our sufferings and our loneliness. Psalm 77 is a good psalm for helping us to learn this form of prayer which is the act of remembering the miracles of the past done by God. This should give us hope for the future as it did for the people of Israel.

**Psalm
78**
ॐ

This psalm is classified as historical; it is also didactic, for it teaches the importance of learning the history of God's actions among God's chosen people Israel. The pattern so common to the Torah is present in this psalm as it recalls the mighty acts of God. The giving of the covenant, then failure, repentance, and a return to the covenant are seen in the ebb and flow of God's history with Israel. This psalmist narrates in great detail the marvels of the Exodus and continues the pilgrimage of Israel into the land of Canaan, and finally ends with the reign of David as king under God. Thus a period of time extending from 1200 to 1000 B.C.E. is the scope of this psalm. The poet encourages the community gathered in the Temple to pass on the presence of God to their children and to future generations. It is a history of their traditions and life with God as leader. This excellent storyteller may be a priest or a Levite concerned with the worship in the Temple.

The opening verses (1 to 4) are similar to the message of Deuteronomy 32 and recall the covenant God makes with the people of Israel (verses 5 through 9). Despite the covenant and the miracles worked, Israel falls back on its promises. This is especially seen in the strong tribe of Ephraim and then of Joseph. Their deceit and stubborn rebellion bring about their rejection by God. God had guided them through the desert with the pillar of fire and the cloud — visible manifestations of God's power and guidance. They do not learn from the plagues inflicted upon Egypt, nor from the manna and the quail given in the desert. Despite all of these marvels, "they still sinned" (verse 22). Yet, the Holy One of Israel continues to show them compassion and forgives them. The above pattern of renewal, return, and failure sets in time and time again. They do not learn from past experiences. The psalmist continues to hammer this home, hoping they will learn and teach the future generations this great lesson of God's fidelity and protection throughout their history.

The poet weaves in and out of the Exodus narrative, that of Numbers, and Deuteronomy. He is teaching wisdom and covenant responsibilities from these words of God; he himself is a wisdom figure. He recalls the plagues to make his point not, however, in the same order or number as given in Exodus 7-12. Reread verses 42-51.

The psalmist continues the instruction in salvation history as Israel is led into the promised land of Canaan (verses 52-55), having always the same intention, namely that Israel should learn from its past history and from the perennial covenant that was made with *YHVH* given at Sinai through Moses. As the history continues, the northern tribes remain obdurate; their shrine at Shiloh is abandoned by God (verse 60). The wisdom lyricist then takes us through the time of the Judges (verses 56-66). Finally, God awakens like a warrior from a deep sleep, routs the adversaries and rejects Ephraim and Joseph. Now Judah and David take center stage for God's loving concern and guidance. Mount Zion, David, and Jerusalem are signs and symbols of God's strength among the people. God and the poet continue the instruction and exhort them to remain faithful and to remember the covenant made now with David, who is the shepherd for the flock of God, having been himself chosen from the life of a shepherd, and who now reigns as king.

My personal reflection on this psalm leads me to see and experience the pedagogy of God. The psalm helps me to learn the lessons of God's salvation history. The marvels of the Exodus are powerful manifestations of God's love. I want to have a listening heart to realize this is true also for us in our history. By listening and obeying God's command, I, too, can be a person of wisdom who passes on the message of God's eternal love and care. We all are teachers of wisdom from our own experiences of God, and we can learn much from our present psalm. I conclude my reflection with a great insight given to me from a spiritual book on the psalms. The author tells us that the rabbis were aware of 5896 words in the psalms, and right in the middle of the Psalter is verse 38 from the psalm we are pondering. We enter the heart of God as we read the verse: "Yet, He, being merciful, forgave their sin and destroyed them not; often He turned back His anger and let none of His wrath be roused" (Dollen, 131).

Psalm 79

This is a national and/or community lamentation. The pathos and tenor of the psalm makes the period of the Exile just after the destruction of the city of Jerusalem fit the outcry and lamentation of the psalmist who leads the people in prayer. The Babylonian exile lasted from 587-537 B.C.E. The fresh memories of the destruction of Jerusalem and the defilement of their holy places make this psalm one of the more graphic and vivid ones in the Psalter. The remains of the unburied witnesses disturb us as we read and ponder the occasion for the outcry. This non-burying is an abomination that cries out to the Lord because of the shedding of blood of the innocent and of God's people. The first four verses are a vivid recollection of this devastating period. Verses 5-10 are a plea for God to take vengeance upon the "nations." Verse 8 is the breakthrough that leads to the heart of the prayer: "Remember not against us the iniquities of our forefathers; let Thy compassion speedily come to meet us, for we are brought very low." In verse 9 there are themes and words similar to the prayer that Jesus taught his disciples: "Help us, O God of our salvation, for the sake of the glory of Thy name; and deliver us, and forgive our sins, for Thy name's sake." Verses 11-13 express hope for the future and thanksgiving to God for deliverance in the past.

This psalm and Psalm 137 are used in the liturgy of the synagogue for the Ninth Day of Av (*Tish'ah be-Av*) which commemorates the anniversary of the destruction of the First and Second Temples, the expulsion of the Jewish people from Spain in 1492, and the outbreak of World War I. "One *Tish'ah be-Av*, Napoleon is said to have passed a synagogue and seen people chanting and wailing. On being told why, he explained, 'A people that mourns such an ancient national destruction is entitled to have hope for a national reconstruction'" (Glinert, 244).

The mocking of "the nations" (the term used throughout for the enemy) is a sacrilegious act against God. The taunts and ridicule that the people of God undergo is most humiliating for them. In verse 12 God is asked to fill the folds of the enemies' garments with vengeance as payback for what has been done to God's heritage and name. This brings the psalmist to cry out, "How long, O God, can this continue?" And the response of the taunters counters with, "Where is your God!"

Certainly prayer of this type is heard today after the effects of so many terrorist acts upon other nations. Prayer needs to be this way under such circumstances. The intensity is overwhelming and God is invoked in desperation. On many buses today we see this prayer calling upon the people with signs saying, "United we stand!" This psalm helps us to pray whenever we feel such attacks from the terrorists. We cry out and ask God to settle accounts with such oppressors and murderers.

Psalm 80

🝆

This community and national lamentation contains rich imagery and remarkable descriptions for the stages of God's actions among the people of Israel. These actions we call "salvation history" (*Heilsgeschichte*). This psalmist, one designated as belonging to the Asaph psalmists, is a talented and creative poet. By using a refrain three times and another subtle hint of the same refrain, the psalmist unifies the work while having the community sing or chant the response. It is a cultic celebration at a common shrine, probably a shrine from the northern kingdom such as Shiloh or Bethel.

The structure of the psalm is clear and simple: (1) the plea and outcry in prayer of the people (verses 2-4); (2) the plight of Israel seen in the four mentioned tribes: Joseph, Ephraim, Benjamin, and Manasseh (verses 5-8); (3) remembrance of the saving actions of God in the past through Exodus (verses 9-14); and (4) the prayer of renewed trust in the God of the covenant who is their only hope.

Three stages in Israel are mentioned in this psalm through the imagery used. God is seen as shepherd who led them through the wilderness into the land of promise. Then God is imaged as a vine planter and developer who takes care to cultivate the roots of the people from the sea to the river Euphrates. The settlement of Israel in the promised land is depicted through the cultivation of a vine. Finally, the horrific third stage of the people who have been attacked by the Assyrians from the north (734-721 B.C.E.). The latter represents the time and social location of the psalmist and his community. Most likely Hosea (732-724 B.C.E.) was the king of the northern kingdom at this time. Now only the powerful right arm of Yahweh can bring the people back to the promised land in peace and security.

Personally, in this psalm and the others that are being presented, I attempt to pray and focus on what I consider the heart of the psalm. With a listening and pondering with the heart of my prayer I attempt to apply its lesson to my personal and communitarian prayer. In this psalm I found that the repeated refrain was at the heart of this prayer. It is given possibly four times in the psalm (verses 4, 8, [15] and 20). "God, restore us; and cause Thy face to shine, and we shall be saved." The exegete Leopold Sabourin discovers the refrain to be the message: "In this refrain, the meaning of the whole psalm is condensed, as well as the main object of supplication in all the national laments: a return to normal relations between Yahweh and the covenant people" (Sabourin, 306).

The psalm recalls to mind the beautiful priestly benediction taken from the Book of Numbers 6:24-26: "The Lord bless you and keep you; the Lord make his face to shine upon you, and be gracious to you; the Lord lift up his countenance upon you and give you peace." In this psalm the face of God is called upon to shine on us. This brings the light of God's countenance into our lives as we seek God through this psalm. Certainly the countenance of God is a great way of calling to mind the presence of God in our personal and communitarian prayer.

Psalm

81

♍

This psalm is classified as a liturgical and community celebration of God's fidelity and is the most significant in this category. Other psalms belonging to this genre are 78, 95, 105, 106, and possibly 50 because of its content. Psalm 81 moves through the opening verses from the people of Israel, to the Levites, and then to the priests chanting its celebrations of God's faithfulness throughout the history of God's people. Though some scholars would attach this psalm to the Passover, it seems, in my opinion to fit better the Feast of Booths (*Sukkot*). The mention of the blowing of the shofar or ram's horn and the phases of the moon lead many scholars to associate it with harvest time.

God speaks directly to the people through an oracle probably sung by the priest or a Levite. The liberation of the Israelites from Egypt is recalled; Joseph (Israel) is released from his bonds and from the baskets bearing bricks. This is done in a colorful and descriptive way in the psalm. Other historical saving events besides the Exodus are recalled as the psalm continues.

The psalm consists of two parts: verses 1-5a is a liturgical hymn, while the second part, verses 5b-16, is the oracle emanating from the ark of the covenant in the Temple. The theophany recalls the giving of the Torah on Mount Sinai and the commandments. Thus a salvation history is celebrated throughout the song. Nature and grace are embracing one another in the verses. The moon and the people are interacting while joyfully celebrating the new harvest. God is ever faithful and wants the people to listen to their story of how mercy and fidelity are their gifts from *YHVH*, their God. The decalogue recalls responsibility that is theirs as the people of God. They rejoice, pray, and offer God thanksgiving in this central festival of Israel celebrated in the Temple.

There are occasions in which we too celebrate, sing, and rejoice, for example, a birthday, a bar mitzvah, a bat mitzvah, or a wedding or an anniversary. This psalm shows us the beauty of joining such celebrations to a prayer of thanksgiving to God who created us and the beautiful world within which we live. This psalm is quite appropriate to pray on such occasions or on a jubilee celebration.

Psalm 82

This is a public lamentation, or as M. Dahood says, a prophetic liturgy of God's judgment upon the pagan gods. The word used for the pagan gods is *elohim* and this becomes the key to how one interprets the psalm. *Elohim* is a plural form that can mean three different entities; first, about God as being above the "gods" or *elohim* of the nations; second, as the angels or messengers of God; and third, as human judges who have a divine aura about them through their authority over the poor and the fatherless, the oppressed, and the disabled. Most scholars take the first interpretation and say that this psalm shows God as lording it over all of these gods or divinities in the heavenly court. The rabbinic tradition favors the interpretation of God as judging the human persons who have the authority of judges in society. I tend to agree with this third interpretation and I leave aside the minority but ingenious opinion, of associating this with the messengers or angels of God who are misusing their powers. Fortunately, no matter which of the three one prefers, the conclusion is the same, namely, that God is the supreme judge and all others are called to account for their poor judgments made at the expense of ordinary humans or the poor of *YHVH*.

The psalm is logical and simple in its development. Verse 1 describes God as the supreme judge over all other judges. Verses 2-4 state that God's just judgment will vindicate the poor, the fatherless, and the oppressed. Verses 5-7 show how the "unjust gods, angels, or human judges" are convicted and even given the death sentence by the supreme judge, God. Verse 8 is a prayer in which the psalmist appeals to the justice of God in judging the people. Verses 1 and 8 form an inclusion and make this a straightforward, compact, and unified literary piece.

It is noted by the scholars that Jesus in the Fourth Gospel cites verse 6 of this psalm which is also a key to its interpretation. Jesus says, "Is it not written in your law, 'I said, ye are gods?'" (John 10:34). This links Jesus with an interpretation similar to the rabbinic one.

I think this psalm speaks to me as a counselor and teacher. It also is addressed to those in leadership positions like judges, representatives of the people, clergy, and lawyers. These people are held in esteem by those who place their trust in them. The betrayal of this trust and the misuse of authority can be devastating for the client, pupil, or friend. This situation can only be remedied by the divine judgment of God on those who have misused their gifts at the expense of others. This is especially to be watched carefully in those leaders of affluent countries, but no one is exempt from the honesty and integrity called for in these positions. I was impressed with this saying from the "Ethics of the Fathers" (*Pirqei Avot*). "By three things is the world preserved: by truth, by judgment, and by peace." The saying is probably contemporary to Rabbi Hillel and Rabbi Akiva of the first century.

**Psalm
83
🎵**

This psalm is a community and national lamentation or prayer for divine help. It happens to be the last of the Asaph collection of psalms (named after the ancestor of the Levites who composed such psalms for the Temple). The word "name" is a key to interpreting this psalm. We do see something similar to a curse psalm as we get into the second part of this poem, but the final verse is a prayer that the adversaries may have a change of heart and then have respect for both God's and Israel's name. Thus rather than retaliation or vindictiveness, the psalm is a prayer beseeching God Most High to be revered and known by the nations.

Verses 2-6 are strong addresses to God to cease from being silent, still, and calm about what is happening to Israel, God's chosen possession and people. Ten attackers or oppressors are named as we move through the psalm. The Nations are intent on blotting out the very name of God by erasing that of Israel. The word "name" indicates the person and the essential reality of Israel. Verses 7-19 list the nations and cities and peoples who are raging against Israel. This leads the psalmist to pray for their overthrow of those who are compared to a tumultuous, rioting crowd (verse 3).

We have seen how difficult it is to place the psalms chronologically. Scholars range from the monarchy all the way to the second century before the Common Era, a period of some eight hundred years. The same is true for this psalm which cannot be assigned to one specific period in the history of Israel. Some of the enemies were dealt with by David (the Edomites, Ishamaelites, and Philistines); others pertain to succeeding times of warfare under lesser kings than David. As we look at the locations indicated by the names of the oppressors we see that all of the country is being involved in war and surrounded

by the enemy. The Soncino commentary wisely says, "The saf-
est line to take is to see the poem as an amalgam of history and
poetry" (Cohen, 272).

Though the psalm is difficult to pray and listen to by
today's readers, it does help us understand how essential God's
presence and providence are to a people who have always been
under attack. God takes care of the treasured Israel with a
mantle of protection. Oesterly, one of the great interpreters of
the psalms, remarks about the difficulty of a cursing psalm: "If
we cannot approve, we may understand; if we had been where
the psalmist was, we might well have felt and spoken as he did"
(Cohen, 273). C.S. Lewis has a good insight for handling the
cursing parts of psalms. He suggests we personalize the enemies
as our own battles with sin, insincerity, and wrongdoing. These
have to be cursed and fought against throughout our life. Only
a strong desire and a powerful plea made to God can help us
overcome our selfishness and our willingness to give in to temptations at the expense of our neighbors. Personal victory is only
assured through the grace and assistance of God whose name
is to be sacredly invoked.

*Psalm
84*
❧

This psalm is a canticle of Zion sung on the
occasion of a pilgrimage to the Temple during the time of the first soft rainfall and harvest. This fits well the festivities of Tabernacles during the month of September or
October. The reference to anointing is an
indication that the feast could also be an annual celebration of the king's accession to the
throne. Like the other psalms in the collection of psalms attributed to the sons of Korah, it is a masterpiece of imagery, sym-

bolism, and literary beauty. The feelings, impressions, and joys of a pilgrim are experienced as one reads and meditates on this song. This is the psalm par excellence for a pilgrimage or a visit to a special sacred place like a synagogue or the Temple. The psalmist shared his feelings and his joy upon reaching the Temple on Mount Zion during the harvest feast of Tabernacles.

The structure consists of three equal stanzas which blend together in harmonic simplicity and clarity of expression. In the original Hebrew text the stanzas are easily recognized by the use of the word *selah* which indicates a stop or pause in the psalm which calls for either a new melody or a return to the original music after an interlude. The *selah* appears in verse 5 and verse 9 which gives the composition a marvelous balance in lines and words.

In the first stanza (verses 2-5) we experience the psalmist's yearning to reach Mount Zion and the Temple for worship, celebration, and joyful singing. Verses 6-9 are the second stanza and they tell of the journey to Jerusalem and how its difficulties are surmounted because of the desire and burning heart to reach its goal. Finally, the last stanza (verses 10-13) are expressions of wonder, joy and praise of the Lord God of Hosts.

Three times within this psalm a beatitude is expressed for the one going to God's dwelling place (verses 5, 6, and 13). God is addressed four times as the Lord God of Hosts (verses 2, 4, 9, and 13).

Two of the most beautiful lines within this psalm are found in verses 3 and 12: "My soul yearneth, yea pineth for the courts of the Lord; my heart and my flesh sing for joy unto the living God." And, "For a day in Thy courts is better than a thousand; I had rather stand at the threshold of the house of my God, than to dwell in the tents of wickedness."

I found this psalm helpful for my own personal prayer and my spiritual journey toward God. It stirs up my heart and my devotion while visiting a sacred place where I may experience the presence and grace and glory of God (verse 12). And do we not need such sentiments while on pilgrimage? This psalm makes this a journey of the heart to God's dwelling place. Entering into the heart of this psalm helps us become spiritual pilgrims. I was privileged several times to treasure this psalm as such a pilgrim even though the person who composed it lived almost three thousand years ago.

Psalm 85 ❦

This is a community lamentation which is easily accommodated to the historical return of Israel to its homeland during the more benign rule of Cyrus the Great of Persia during the years after 582 B.C.E. There are some commentators, M. Dahood among them, who would make the psalm pre-exilic because of the ancient tone seen in its vocabulary. But the sentiments expressed within the verses and the imagery used are more resonant with the return motif and the hope of rebuilding the Temple for worship and song. In rereading the prophet Haggai, I found a helpful insight into the mood for this epoch of Israel. The superscription tells us it is a psalm from the Korahite collection (Psalms 42, 44-49). This psalm would then be a prayer sung by or led by a Levite whose ancestry is bound up with Korah. There is a psalm which also has the same tone about it but is not from the family of the Korahites, namely, Psalm 126, one of the ascent psalms. I find these psalms of Korah to have a distinctive literary quality about them and personally a pleasing and attractive imagery and sound.

The psalm helps me understand that Israel is a people, a land, the Torah, and a community of God. There is a wholesome spirit within this people and its relationship to God that is seen within the psalm. These essential ideas come to mind as one reads the first four verses. The composer has a skillful way of matching the verses with similar sounds as well as the characteristic parallelism used in Hebrew poetry.

In the schema of salvation history even a foreign ruler like Cyrus serves in accomplishing God's will for the people of Israel. The return is due to his provident foresight and wisdom. In a sense, he participates in the messianic role that a king should have.

As the psalm continues we enter into the lamentation verses 5 through 7. This is the complaint of the psalmist that God should cease from being angry. Then a powerful prayer breaks the complaint in verse 8: "Show us Thy mercy, O Lord, and grant us Thy salvation." God is asked to continue this mercy and to refrain from any further burning indignation against Israel. Then peace and righteousness shall meet and kiss in the land of Israel. The prophetic voice of the priest or Levite then announces that salvation and glory will dwell in the land to which they return. Yes, "Mercy and truth are met together; righteousness and peace have kissed each other" (verse 11).

The last verses of this psalm continue the imagery and personification of God's qualities seen in mercy and forgiveness and reflected in nature between heaven and earth. God prepares a propitious path for Israel's reentry into Jerusalem.

I pray the psalms every day and upon reflecting about this particular psalm I realized how much I like it as a prayer in times of restoration of energy, a return from a long and tiring trip, or in a transforming change happening in my life. I have come to appreciate in a special way the genius of the Korahite psalms, finding them quite poetic, rich in imagery and sound, and delightful to recite. These ancient forms of prayer are released into today's climate because of their symbolism and poetry which is so flexible and malleable, so easily adapted to our mentality.

Certainly this psalm is an excellent one for immigrants and for people returning home after a long journey. I think of a young couple whose wedding I witnessed who moved to France because of work possibilities and due to the fact that the groom is French. I know both are eager to see each other's families, but are equally eager to return to an aging grandfather and the bride's parents. This psalm may be of some comfort to them. It may help us, too, in our prayer to turn our hearts to God and away from ourselves.

Psalm 86 ॐ

This psalm is an individual lamentation according to the scholars, but the simple designation that it is a prayer is the one I prefer, for this is the way the superscription reads. This composition consists of three parts: (1) verses 1-7 show how prayer from a pious individual leads to the appreciation of God's graciousness, mercy and goodness; (2) verses 8-10 are a hymn extolling the universal power of God; (3) verses 11-17 inform us of what is being prayed for by the psalmist. There is a desire to lead a holy and good life and to beg God for help against the proud and the mighty oppressors.

Though scholars tend to think this psalm is simply a repetition of phrases from other psalms, I believe it has the originality of a good prayer coming from the heart of the poet. It is an excellent psalm of pure and simple prayer from a person who is burning with love for God and who centers all of his thoughts on God. God's loving-kindness, mercy, beneficence and grace to the psalmist are sensed throughout the song. I found this one of the easiest psalms to pray and discovered it helps me return to the fundamentals of prayer without getting bogged down with complicated information.

The psalmist centers upon God throughout, calling God *YHVH* (*Adonai* is the preferred pronunciation when reading this sacred name; this means Lord) seven times. This is the most use of the tetragrammaton (*YHVH*) in any psalm. Seven is the number for fullness and certainly this is the desire of the one praying this psalm in the Temple whether it be a humble servant of the Lord (the poet thus identifies himself in verse 1-2) or the king, as some scholars think. The confidence and optimism of this prayer is sensed throughout taking away, in my estimation, the lamenting which is rather faint. In this prayer there is perseverance, humility, and absolute trust in the Lord. Prayer, after all, is neither a study of someone else's words, nor an exegetical exercise, nor research into history. We join in this psalm, lifting our hearts and minds to the Lord (*YHVH*) who created us. This psalm serves as prayer for those who are more intellectually inclined, leading them into prayer that comes from the heart — a listening heart. As the Christian Hebraist, A.F. Kirkpatrick remarks about this psalm, "It claims no poetic originality, yet it possesses a pathetic earnestness and tender grace of its own" (Cohen, 280).

*Psalm
87*

This is the most beautiful of the songs of
Zion, a hymn of praise to God who has
founded and blessed Zion. It is cherished
both for its message of universality which
gives each one that sense of belonging in a
special way to God and for its profound religious spirit. Zion is the homeland and mother
of all nations, races, and peoples. Zion is the
source and wellspring of all blessings that come from God. God
loves her and declares glorious things about her.

Since this is such a short psalm, it lends itself to a concen-
trated reflection and prayer. I enter into its spirit easily and rel-
ish its enticing and encouraging message. For the Gentiles it is
wonderful news and reminds me of what Pope Pius XI said:
"Spiritually we are all Semites."

In contemporary Judaism Zion is a symbol of strength and
unity for the State of Israel. Together with the fortress of
Masada it is at the heart of the people of Israel and their allegiance is symbolized by this ancient name for Jerusalem. Its
prophetic message in the psalm extends to all nations who belong to the Creator God.

In some years past I received a *Tanakh* from a friend and
I admired the creative artistic calligraphy inscribed on the cover
of this Hebrew Bible. It is a citation from Isaiah 2:2-3: "For instruction shall come forth from Zion, the word of the Lord from
Jerusalem." This is at the heart of Psalm 87 and is consonant
with what the seven verses are saying.

Even the enemies of Israel will eventually come to respect
Zion. In an excellent book on the psalms from a Christian perspective, Monsignor Dollen comments on the nations mentioned in the psalm: "The glorious things that were said of
Jerusalem were based on the fact that it was the center of worship of the one, true God. All flowed from that. Because of that,

all nations were invited into the fold, an especially forthright understanding of the universality of the call to all the nations, even those who were formerly enemies — Babylon, Egypt (Rahab), Philistia, Ethiopia (Cush) and Tyre — to worship God" (Dollen, 153).

In meditating and pondering over this psalm we are led to think of many of the prophetic words uttered in the *Tanakh* (Isaiah 2:2-4; 54:1-3; 60:3-9; Ezekiel 37:28; Amos 9:11s.; Micah 4:1-3) and in the New Testament (Galatians 4:26).

The psalm helps us center directly upon God who has chosen Zion as a sacred location for all peoples, races, and nations. God remembers, however, that it is essentially the possession of Israel, God's chosen people. While continuing our prayer it is good to turn to the other songs of Zion: Psalms 46, 48, 76, and 132.

Psalm
88
🜨

This psalm is described by most commentators as the saddest within the whole collection of 150 psalms. It is a profound and agonizing lamentation of an individual whether that be one of the "poor of *YHVH*" or one of the kings of Judah named Azariah (Uzziah who lived in the eighth century before the Common Era). This king was afflicted with leprosy towards the end of his life. The psalm throughout describes the agony one goes through at the hour of death. Verse 16 implies that the lamentation comes from a person who was afflicted with an illness from youth. These are the two possibilities to choose from.

The psalm is divided into three stanzas: (1) an outcry to the Lord God (*YHVH-Elohim*) in which the suffering person describes his situation; (2) verses 11-13 is a direct imploring of

God for help though the sufferer feels alone and abandoned; (3) finally, there is a renewal of his prayer for help in verses 14-19 while continuing contact with God despite a situation that seems utterly hopeless. The struggle to live is up against all odds for survival.

In many respects this is a poem that is similar to the ordeals of Job. The description of death and Sheol (the underworld) is expressed 17 times with most vivid phrases and words. In this respect, we have the most descriptive ideas of Sheol in the whole Bible. The scholar of psalms, Oesterley, states that this lamentation "is written with the very heart's blood of the poet" (Cohen, 285).

Despite the dreadful thick description of the piece about a man near death, there is the evidence that this person continues to live in the presence of God with an I-Thou form of prayer and lament. Is this not like our own personal experience where some suffering or tragedy affects us and we feel totally abandoned by everyone, perhaps, even by God? We are up against the wall and are forced in our pain to return to God in prayer, remembering the All Holy One who alone can rescue us. In this moment, Psalm 88 matches our feelings and emotions which lead us to resonate with this sad lamentation. I think this is an honest form of prayer. God is not dead and we know it. We continue to hope against hope and to express our desolation to God who is commanded to listen to our plea. Like the psalmist we do not reject the existence of God even though we do not see any change in our situation or in our misery. We continue our prayer like this sad soul and in so doing there is a spark of hope. Death itself is a part of the human experience, and praying in the hour of death is also a very human thing to do and so we, too, cry out for help: "O Lord, God of my deliverance, when I cry out in the night before You, let my prayer reach You; incline your ear to my cry" (verses 3-4).

Psalm 89

This is one of the longer psalms in the Psalter and is classified as a royal psalm said within a community of worship on a festival dealing with both God as king and the servants of God who are kings in the Davidic lineage. The psalm is a profound reflection on the historical event of the anointing of David as king (2 Samuel 7:8-16) without, however, being the actual situation of David's kingship. It can be applied to all Davidic kings as a cultic prayer. More than the other royal psalms, this one focuses on the magnificent covenant relationship that God has with God's anointed ones. We learn much about the nature of God in covenantal love with Israel through this psalm.

Most scholars break the psalm into three to five parts. I prefer Dahood's division and that of the Latin translation which has five stanzas. Within the psalm the themes are repeated both through covenant terminology and through other linguistic similarities in the words and phrases. It is best to leave the psalm untouched; it is a unit that makes sense in the light of a cultic celebration of both good times and bad times for the Davidic dynasty. Part I is a prelude (verses 2-5) in which the theme of covenant theology is evident. Part II extols the absolute power of God over all of creation; this is a magnificent cosmogony (verses 6-19). Part III is a prophetic oracle proclaimed by the Temple priest which shows the covenant that was originally established through David (2 Samuel 7:14). Part IV is the king's lamentation and that of the nation during a difficult time of defeat and humiliation for the nation. Part V is simply added to end the collection of book three of the psalms with a familiar doxology and the twofold reiteration, "Amen, Amen!"

The prelude addresses God as *YHVH* and this continues throughout the psalm as the preferred name for God. God has

"cut" a covenant of love (*ḥesed*) and fidelity with his chosen one,
David, the anointed messiah king of Judah. This covenant is
always characterized by God's ever faithful love (the words used
in Hebrew are *ḥesed* and *emunah*). These descriptive words will
be repeated eight times throughout the psalm. Several other attributes will be added, too, and these are loving-kindness,
fidelity, justice, and solid rock truth. The covenant is enhanced
within the context of salvation history for Israel, God's chosen
people. In the first half of the psalm it seems the Golden Age of
David and Solomon is recalled and celebrated in the Temple
festivities for the renewal of the king's enthronement. Verse 19
serves as a summary of what is central to the celebration: "Indeed *YHVH* is truly our shield, the Holy One of Israel, is truly
our king." I see verse 15 as the heart of the psalm: "Justice and
true judgment are the foundation of Thy throne, love and
friendship go before Thee."

Suddenly the tone changes and this poem of hope becomes
one of disappointment seen in the king's prayer. It also represents the consternation of the people or nation of Judah and Israel. The king asks, "Why is this happening to us now, O God?
Why have you rejected us and your covenant with us?" This is
a traumatic experience for a devoted king like David who calls
God his Father and who considers himself as the firstborn son.
We see this in verse 27: "Thou art my Father, my God and the
rock of my salvation." How can defeat and the taunts from oppressors (and even from some of the people) happen to us when
we were so closely knit in the love and fidelity of you and us in
the covenant? Is it possible that your covenant is irrevocable
when these things are happening? "Where are Thy former mercies, O Lord, which Thou didst swear unto David in Thy faithfulness?"

This psalm touched me personally and helped me understand the love God had for his beloved David. The rupture,

however, that is felt by the psalmist strikes me like an experiencing of losing a best friend or a lover. We all experience this whenever a deep relationship with another comes to an end. Hope changes to disappointment and even to anger. We are numbed and forsaken while still hoping for a reconciliation which does not occur. Yes, even though the psalm is chanted as a national hymn it touches the individual leader or king. We sense his feelings and his pain.

It seems that only renewed faith in God is able to bring the psalmist some consolation. This is what we sense in the final line of the psalm, "Blessed be the Lord forever more. Amen. Amen."

Psalm 90 ৡ

This psalm is a community lamentation. The superscription reads that it was composed by Moses. This has been maintained in the rabbinic tradition and makes some sense since there is a unique wisdom-like tone similar to what is found in the Book of Deuteronomy in chapters 32 and 33. Verses 7-12 also seem to be a reflection of the difficult time the Israelites had while wandering in the desert and of their sinfulness during this period. The psalm has been captured in Isaac Watts' hymn entitled, "O God, Our Help in Ages Past."

In the first verse God is addressed as "Lord" through the Hebrew word *Adonai* and it appears in verse 17 as well. This forms what is called an inclusion and points to the unity of the poem, even though the sacred name *YHVH* is pointed with vowels taken from the Hebrew word for Lord (*Adonai*). In this psalm, the sacred name *YHVH* is not used and the word *Adonai* stands by itself as a separate name for God.

Psalm 90

The wisdom motif of the poem centers on the unlimited and eternal nature of God as contrasted with the limits of humans whose years are like a sigh, or like flood waters passing by, or even like the short-lived grass which sprouts in the morning but wilts at eventide. Mortals last seventy years or, if they are strong, they may reach eighty. God, however, is eternal and a thousand years are like yesterday in God's eternity.

As the psalm moves on we find that the wise person understands the mortality of the human race and offers a plea that God should balance the limits and difficult times with as many good things and blessings. The psalmist says, "Make us glad according to the days wherein Thou hast afflicted us according to the years wherein we have seen evil" (verse 15).

As we have seen, the human heart with its desires has a large part to play within the psalms. Since this psalm emphasizes the wisdom motif, we hear the following: "Teach us to count up the days that are ours, and we shall come to the heart of wisdom" (NJB). Moses had this type of wisdom, for in his exhortation he proclaims, "If they were wise, they would understand this, they would discern their latter end" (Deuteronomy 32:29).

These thoughts from the psalm make me thankful for each day of life that I enjoy. Its perspective helps me appreciate life in all of its moments and in its fullness, while recognizing how fragile and how quickly life moves on. Very few of us reach the century mark in years, hence, we follow that practical advice of "taking one day at a time." In so doing, we touch a bit of the wisdom of this psalm. Like the psalmist it is wise to ask for God's blessings and graces each day that we awaken. "May the sweetness of the Lord be upon us, to confirm the work we have done" (verse 17, NJB).

Psalm
91
༃

This is a psalm of great confidence in God; a didactic wisdom psalm that teaches what absolute trust in God is all about. The rewards of such confidence are security and protection for the faithful and trusting person. The psalm is a literary masterpiece in its colorful expressions, its unity, and its contrasts (Hebrew parallelism). The use of all three singular personal pronouns within it testify that it was used in the Temple as part of a liturgical and festive celebration. There is an alternation of the verses through the use of the pronouns that makes it quite pleasant and rhythmic in its presentation. The Talmud has a creative interpretation for the psalm in that it says David is the one speaking in verses 2-8, with a response from Solomon in verse 9, and then, the priest in verse 10 gives an oracle which is that of God's voice for the congregation and the king or the person praying.

The names given to God in this poem are the Most High (*Elyon*), the Almighty (*Shaddai*), He who is our Lord (*YHVH*), and the God above all other "gods" (*Elohim*). The poet uses contrasting colorful imagery from the world of light and darkness, the animal world, the world of fowl, and finally the angelic realm. This is marvelously accomplished through the characteristic Hebrew parallelism of thought that is used in most psalms. One sometimes can understand a line by reading the very next line which expresses the same idea in different words. Confidence is the theme that continues from start to finish in this psalm. The one praying becomes aware more and more of the protective power of God as the poem moves on. Neither pestilence, nor snares or traps, nor wild animals or sea serpents, nor war can harm God's faithful one. All of the gloom and fears of the last psalm (90) are offset in the absolute trust in God in this piece.

For the reader it is best to consider this psalm as having two parts: verses 1-13 are filled with didactic wisdom which inspires confidence, while part two is the promise and protection that has been promised and effected now by God.

In studying and reflecting on this psalm and on the other psalms, I try to get at the heart of the message by attuning my own heart and mind to the central ideas of the psalm. I attempt to have a listening heart (*lev shome'a*) for what the poet is saying. In being attuned to this psalm I found that verse 11 speaks to my heart and soul: "For He (*YHVH*) will give His angels charge over thee, to keep thee in all thy ways" and then in part two: "Because he has set his love upon Me (*YHVH*), therefore will I deliver him; I will set him on high, because he hath known my Name." I personally use this psalm as a night prayer and feel that it would also be an excellent one for children to hear and listen to at bedtime.

Psalm 92
🍂

This is a thanksgiving hymn. It stems from the time of the Second Temple and was probably composed by one of the Levites — those who spent days and nights in Temple service and worship. In Judaism the psalm is recited on the Sabbath; this is also what the superscription indicates in the text. The Targum on this psalm says that Adam composed this in thinking about God's wonderful creation.

The first six verses of this psalm are a wonderful paean of praise and thanksgiving to God the Almighty and the One who is (*YHVH*). This praise is both sung and accompanied by musical instruments. This indicates that it is in the time of the more developed psalmody used in the Temple with all sorts of stringed instruments. Verse 3 is at the heart of this part of the psalm: "To declare Thy loving-kindness in the morning, and Thy faithfulness in the night seasons." The two words used for the attributes of God, *hesed* and *emunah* are translated as loving-kindness and faithfulness; these are also at the heart of the covenant God has made with Israel. Verses 5 and 6 are marvelous tributes to the creation and work of God now finished as the Sabbath is celebrated.

A wise and wholesome person honors God in this manner, while a fool and a brute is not aware of the goodness of God's presence in creation (verses 7-10). In the remaining verses, this hymn seems to emphasize God's gifts to the king who also praises God in the Temple. The symbol of the horn is that of the strength of the king, while the anointing shows that the king is God's elect, his messiah. The continued contrast of the righteous with the wicked is evident. The former is like the palm tree or the cedar of Lebanon, while the latter is simply like the withering grass of the fields. The final line of the psalm is a doxology of the righteousness of God thus summing up the praise of the Creator by the psalmist.

This psalm makes me feel at peace with God as I am led through its first five or six verses. Honor and praise are given to the Creator and as I continue to pray, read, or study the psalm, I am encouraged to live a good, honest, and wholesome life based on God's love, kindness, and fidelity. There is also a gentle warning not to be brutish or foolish in my behavior. It makes the day worth living to have such a positive attitude toward God and all of God's creation. Yes, I was very much at home with this psalm in study, prayer, and reflection.

Psalm 93 ☙

This psalm is classified as a hymn of praise dedicated to God as king. Its theme will be more fully developed in similar "enthronement of *YHVH* psalms" such as Psalms 95-100. Psalm 47 has a similar theme of celebration of *YHVH* as king. The emphasis is on the rule of God over the universe and all peoples. Keep in mind that Psalms 97 and 99 are also closely related to what our present psalm contains. Some scholars link these psalms to those of Zion (Psalms 46, 48, 76, 84, 87, 122).

The structure of the psalm is quite simple. Verse 1 is the introduction stating that God reigns and is clothed with majestic splendor. Verses 2-4 are the body of the psalm describing how God is ruling over the turbulent chaotic and powerful waters. Verse 5 is the conclusion stating that God's rule is holy and trustworthy.

In the superscription of the Septuagint (the Greek translation done around 150 B.C.E.) and in the Talmud, this psalm is assigned to Temple usage on the Friday just before the Sabbath, for it describes God as king over the earth as fully inhabited and completed (Genesis 1:24-31). The psalmist commences with an emphatic use of God's most holy name, *YHVH*. I believe it best to keep the verb in the present tense which emphasizes that the Lord (*YHVH*) is always ruling even though some translate it as "*YHVH* becomes king." Such a translation links the chronology of the psalm to the time after the Babylonian captivity when the Lord would become king once again. The thrust of the psalm shows that *YHVH* always was and is king especially over the primeval powerful chaotic waters. This part of the psalm seems to be an adaptation of the ancient Mesopotamian myth where Marduk is king of the gods and slays Tiamat, the raging and roaring waters. It is now interpreted in our psalm that God is the one who always has reigned over all of the universe and over the peoples. I can go along with the mythic borrowing idea which seems confirmed also by the meter used with these lines about the overwhelming waters (2+2+2 in three stichs). I also see the famous parallelism used in Hebrew poetry here in an ascending and progressive manner wherein the description of the power of water increases as the lines move on. Just as a tidal wave sweeps over the land so, too, did Israel experience the oppression of the heathen powers, but God is their king and God has always reigned over all creation. The conclusion of the poem focuses on the God who is in the Temple and whose throne is the mercy seat resting on the cherubim. This final line balances well with the introduction and shows that God is the center of the worship in the Temple of Jerusalem.

In reflecting on this psalm I sense the great power and majesty of God. The image of a majestic king is the choice of our psalmist and I am led to follow his description of God's powerful reign over the universe and the waters. Believing in God as Creator I am convinced of God's personal and providential concern for all of creation. Nothing is by mere coincidence or chance in the perspective of this psalm. In times of war, natural disasters, and terrorism, the message of this hymn helps us focus on God who has set the world and the universe in its ordered course. Despite the calamities and tragedies that we bring about and that nature too joins at times, they are ultimately part of the divine plan of ongoing creation. I pause and thank God that God rules over all of creation. My response is the same as the psalmist's: "Your decrees stand firm, unshakable; holiness is the beauty of your house, Yahweh, for all time to come" (Psalm 93:5, NJB).

Psalm 94

☙

This psalm is classified as both an individual and a community lamentation. D.G. Castellino's classical commentary on the psalms considers it a wisdom psalm. As in many of the lamentations there is also a thanksgiving section in verses 16-19 indicating that God has heard the complaint of the king or the psalmist who prays in the name of the assembly.

The strong word for "vengeance" is used twice in the opening of the psalm and it is attributed to God, the just judge. Perhaps the psalmist sees God as a judge who renders retributive and social justice in a decisive way. The verse does recall the sentence from Deuteronomy 32:35: "Vengeance is mine, says the Lord."

The reason or cause for the lamentation is taken up in verses 3-7. The unjust and wicked ones, unfortunately, seem to belong to the people of Israel and are not outsiders who are oppressing the orphan, the widow, the stranger. How can God tolerate them and how long will this situation continue? The prophetic tone here reminds us of the prophetic outcry of a Jeremiah or an Amos. Social justice as well as retributive justice is being called forth from the God in whom the people and the psalmist trust.

In verses 8-11 the wicked judges are like brutes from the animal world and fools who lack the wisdom of understanding the laws of the Creator. Their very ears and eyes were fashioned by God but they imagine God does not see their corrupt dealings with their own people and nation. Verse 9 is important here, and A. Cohen states, "He who gave others the power to hear and see can surely Himself hear and see. John Stuart Mill (English philosopher) said that this verse contains the strongest argument for the existence of God" (309).

The next set of verses (12-15) is a transition which turns

to the ones who are wise and know how to follow God's instructions and laws. These people are truly blessed and happy. We
thus have an answer to the query posed whether God would
abandon his people and heritage, Israel (verses 5 and 14). God
alone sustains the people as we see in verses 16-23. Here the
psalmist or the king speaks for the nation and people. The heart
of their prayer is one of thanksgiving; the king expresses this
for the faithful. We hear the psalmist saying, "When I thought,
'My foot is slipping,' your steadfast love, O Lord, held me up.
When the cares of my heart are many, your consolations cheer
my soul" (verses 18-19, NRSV).

The final verses of the psalm are wisdom reflections assur-
ing the assembly of people in the Temple courtyard that God
will exact justice from the crafty and unscrupulous judges who
have distorted the truth and who are criminals when it comes
to justice and mercy. But for the king or the psalmist, God is a
tower of strength and a rock of refuge.

Though verse 20 is considered to be the most difficult and
faulty verse in the psalm, the interpretation offered by A. Cohen
is noteworthy: "Though He may tolerate them for a time, it is
inconceivable that God should let these rapacious judges shel-
ter themselves under His authority" (311).

In reflecting on the image of God in this psalm, I discovered that the sacred Tetragrammaton is used eleven times
(*YHVH* and *Yah*) as well as several variations of the name for
God as *El*. This abundant centering on the person of God who
is the Creator of all that is good and just helps me understand
the strong faith and trust of the psalmist in God. Though he calls
for the vengeance of God, there is really a plea for just retribu-
tion and punishment for those misusing their power as judges.
The presence of God throughout the psalm lets me enter into the
prayer of a faithful one of Israel. I see his heart yearning for the
justice and mercy of God upon his people and nation.

Psalm 95

♱

This psalm is a magnificent and beautiful hymn of praise celebrated in the Temple worship offered to God as king during the festival of the covenant renewal at new year's and harvest time. The liturgical atmosphere is easily sensed in the praise, song, gestures, and honor given to God who is king of all creation and the God who has made a covenant with the assembly of Israel, God's chosen and elected people. The psalm is a call to worship God in the Temple on Mount Zion. It is a perfect psalm for the morning prayer of anyone who worships God.

Attributed to David in the Hebrew tradition, it is most likely a composition done during the time of the Second Temple after the Babylonian exile. Thus it stems from the sixth century before the Common Era.

Twice within the hymn the people are invited to praise and worship God (verses 1, 2 and 6). The reasons for doing this are immediately given: God is supreme over the heights of creation and over the depths of the world. Moreover, God has made a covenant with Israel. He is their God, they are his people. The poet uses the image of the strong hand of God like a shepherd who provides and cares for the flock of his pasture (verse 7).

In the second part of the psalm we have a prophetic exhortation coming from God through the priest admonishing the people not to be like their ancestors who murmured and rebelled at Massah and Meribah (two place names that indicate "strife" and "contention"). Their hearts must not wander and go astray as those who wandered about in the desert for forty years. Otherwise, this present assembly of God (*Qehal YHVH*) will not enter into the "rest" of God, that is, the promised land. Since the word "rest" also recalls the Sabbath, this psalm is used in the sense of the Sabbath rest which God gives the people. This was an interpretation given to the last verse after the sixteenth century.

The psalm makes me think of a legend or midrash that has been shared with me several times. It recalls that God continues to keep the world in order and harmony without destroying it because there are 36 just persons alive on this day. They live out the commandments of God and fulfill the covenantal promises and agreements they made with God. The numerical symbol of the alphabet meaning the number 36 is the name given to these just persons who are called the *lamed-vav* people. In the Soncino commentary, I think Abrahams is saying the same thing: "If Israel observed even one Sabbath according to its true spirit, deliverance would forthwith ensue" (312).

I am in amazement how much is contained within this wonderful hymn of praise. Arthur Weiser in his classic commentary encapsulates this in the following sentence: "The profound meaning of the liturgical festival as an encounter between God and his people finds its fulfillment in the fact that the ancient tradition of the *Heilsgeschichte* regarding creation, election and the making of the covenant at Sinai is here renewed as a present sacral event (cf. of the "today" in v. 7b), and that God's power and saving grace are here revealed before the eyes of his people, who in their turn humble themselves in his presence, offering him their humility and adoration, their gratitude and trust, their submission and obedience" (Weiser, 626).

I personally love this psalm and pray it every morning, saying it in Hebrew and relishing its message with great devotion, attention, and reverence.

Psalm 96

☙

This psalm is a jubilant enthronement hymn to God who is the king who reigns forever. As part of the collection of the enthronement psalms in this fourth book of the Psalter, it has a certain newness and universal invitation to it. In fact, the author or composer is deliberately creating a new song for *YHVH* the King.

The psalm also sends us to chapter 16 of 1 Chronicles which helps us understand and imagine how this and the other psalms were created in both their liturgical settings and in their social location. In this chapter both David and Asaph are mentioned to have a role in the singing and composing of psalms. The particular psalms mentioned are Psalms 105, 106, and our present Psalm 96 on the occasion of the ark's being brought back in jubilant ceremony to Zion. Chronicles actually has the following verses from these three psalms: Psalm 96:1-13 (entire psalm), Psalm 105:1-15; Psalm 106:47-48. T. Butler notes that there are 45 textual differences in 1 Chronicles from the presentation of the Psalter itself (142-50). We are also informed through 1 Chronicles that it was the Levites who were responsible for the liturgical celebrations of the psalms in worship before and during the time of the First and Second Temple. The leading opinion is that this psalm was probably created after the exile for the Second Temple. My purpose in referring the reader to 1 Chronicles is to give the background for the psalms as we know them in the Hebrew Scriptures.

Our psalm is easy to outline. Verses 1-3 are a summons to all peoples to sing and praise God as king. Verses 4-6 show that God alone is supreme and above all other creatures in glory, splendor, and majesty. Verses 7-10 present God as reigning; therefore, praise, adoration, offerings and song are appropriate in our worship of God as king. Verses 11-13 show all of nature attesting to the supremacy of God in judgment and as king. Within the structure of this outline, it is easy to see the "staircase parallelism" in verses 1 and 2, and 7 and 8. The repetitive use of lead words makes this parallelism recognizable.

In this psalm we see the composer centering on the name of God as *YHVH*. It is used 11 times within this hymn. This attests to the theocentric and monotheistic faith of the Levite who composed this poem. All other semblances of the divinity are zeros and nothingness. Only *YHVH* is King and God.

A. Weiser gives us the heart of this psalm in his commentary: "The proclamation of the Kingship of God is linked up with the declaration of the two foundation-pillars of the realization of his salvation — creation and judgment so that the idea of judgment here appears as the sequel to the idea of the universe. The order of Nature in creation and the order of History in judgment are planned by God in such a way that they are turned to each other and supplement each other, being both directed towards their common goal, and that goal is the realization of the 'righteousness of God' in his plan of salvation" (Weiser, 630).

In praying or singing this psalm I am led to a spirit of adoration and reverence of God. Wonder and joy are part of my feelings in reflecting on the words. I am immediately put into the presence of God as Creator of all nature, the universe, the earth, the seas. God is seen as a merciful and kind judge for all of us no matter what our creed, color, or race. I sense the tremendous God-centeredness of this psalm. I am taken out of my own self-awareness and wafted into the greatness of God as supreme king, judge, Creator, and savior. This psalm is filled with such joy and praise that I am exhilarated and grateful for the goodness of my Creator and God who brings all peoples together in worship and awe. God is truly our king and we are called to worship God.

Psalm
97
𐤔

This enthronement hymn to God as king is a combination of traditional pieces from other psalms yet there is also a certain newness to the arrangement. It expresses a strong devotion to *YHVH* as Lord, King, and Judge. The first six verses are a splendid theophany comparable to the great Sinai manifestation of God's presence in the giving of the Torah. There are also similarities to Habakkuk 3:3-12. In the poet's composition there is no doubt about the supremacy of God over the earth and the heavens, and the nothingness of the deities of the nations. God's omnipotence is easily emphasized by the use of God being over all of these realms; in fact, the word "all" (*kol*) is used six times in the psalm. Even the islands are all under God's power.

The second part of the psalm contains the characteristic trait of an enthronement psalm where all of the enemies of Israel are subject to God's almighty power. Verse 9 has a focus on who God is by using one of the oldest expressions used in the history of Jerusalem: "For Thou, Lord (*YHVH*), art most high above the earth; Thou art exalted far above all gods." The title *YHVH Elyon* is used to show the absolute supremacy of God over the heathen deities who are considered "things of naught."

The hymn is eschatological in that it demonstrates God as everlasting and all-powerful both in might and in beneficence. Thus we have both nature (verses 1-6) and history (verses 7-12) balanced within the plan of God and God's powerful reign as King. In the response for the righteous we see God's glory and goodness complemented by the holy ones in God's Temple. The joy, glory, justice and orderliness in creation are constant refrains in this psalm which was celebrated at harvest time and the beginning of the new year when God was proclaimed King. Psalms 47 and 93 had a similar extolling of God who rules over all. A.F. Kirkpatrick, in commenting on this psalm, says that the language of earlier psalmists and prophets are placed into a costly mosaic in this hymn (cited in Cohen, 318).

I am reminded of the gift of hope in our lives when I recite or pray this psalm. Hope resides in our remembering the great things that God has done for us and for those faithful to keeping the commandments of the Torah. These sacred remembrances of God's actions among our ancestors and in our own journeys of life fill us with joy and confidence that God is ever present and loves us with a love beyond all telling. The psalm stirs up a remembrance of God's provident hand in our lives. We treasure these memories as consolations of God and realize once again that the mercies of God come to us each day in the beauty of nature and in the ongoing history of humankind and in our own personal experiences of God's love.

Psalm 98 ❧

This is a hymn of praise to *YHVH* King (an enthronement of God psalm). This is celebrated on the occasion of the new year and thus the psalmist is interested in a "new song" to honor God's supreme reign over Israel and the nations. In many of its phrases it contains the spirit and message of Psalm 96. There are also some striking parallels to Isaiah (chapters 40-66). One can easily see this in Isaiah 40:5; 52:10, 59:16; 63:5). I was especially struck by the verse of Isaiah 52:10 which is almost a perfect parallel to the content of this Psalm 98: "The Lord has bared his holy arm in the sight of all the nations; All the ends of the earth will behold the salvation of our God" (NAB).

The image of God in this hymn is that of a strong king who brings victory to the people of Israel. This is remembered in the Temple and even experienced in a new way; hence, it calls for a new song. The word for victory is also the same one that is used for salvation and it is interchanged in some of the translations in English.

In the three strophes that make up the structure of the hymn, the theme of "call" comes through. Strophe one, verses 1-3, is the call to praise God for the victory granted to Israel. Strophe two, verses 4-6, is a call to the nations to worship God. Strophe three, verses 7-9, calls all creation to worship God the King.

Such universality, which is also characteristic of Isaiah, shows the plan of God at work (*Heilsgeschichte*) in the symbolism for power, the right hand of God and God's outstretched arm; there is also the theme of creation seen through the personification of sea, rivers or floods, and the mountains which join in the praise of God as king. The final strophe centers on the righteousness and equity of God's judgment over all history and creation. Thus an eschatology of hope is seen in this psalm telling us that God's covenant is always faithful and eternal. Covenant terms are easily recognized in the words "mercy" and "faithfulness" (*hesed* and *emunah*) in verse 3.

For me this psalm is light, fast-moving in its expressions, and jubilant. God is an active agent in the victory and the celebration. God reveals, makes known, helps us remember, and reigns as supreme king over nations and nature. I personally enjoyed this psalm; its brisk movement delighted me. It contains the music within its lines that mention the harp, the shofar, the trumpet, and best of all the human voices which join in its jubilancy. It could easily be adopted to a musical concert on the psalms as its prelude. As an aside, I have heard such concerts featuring the composition and singing of new music for the psalms in the synagogues. I am led to join in the chorus and sing a new song to the Lord. I could do no better than sing Psalm 98.

Psalm 99

ॐ

This is a unique enthronement psalm dedicated to the praise of *YHVH* as king of Israel. It clearly emphasizes the holiness and transcendence of God. The call to all nations is not expressed, nor the universalism that was seen in several of the other enthronement psalms. This may indicate an earlier period in the life of Israel, possibly pre-exilic. The holiness of God is easily seen in the conclusion of each of the three stanzas which call to our attention that God is the all-holy one who now reigns as king. The term used for "footstool" may either be the ark of the covenant, Mount Zion, or the Temple. God dwells above them; they are God's footstool. This consistent theme balances some of the irregularities of the psalm in its meter and verses. Despite all of this, the psalm is creative in its expressions and unique as an enthronement psalm. It is the last of them.

The first strophe consisting of verses 1-3 describes God as reigning over all nations, and his rule is mighty and strong. In verse 4 the centrality of Israel is brought out and God displays his justice to the people. The great holy ancestors are Moses, Aaron, and Samuel. They are among those "who called upon the name of the Lord." These are the ones who point to God's holiness and they act as intercessor, priest, prophet, and mediator between God and the people. This is the only psalm in which these three persons are mentioned together.

130

Despite the failures of Israel, God the all-holy one forgives in his loving-kindness and his merciful justice. The people are encouraged to bow down in homage and worship God at his footstool. Verse 3 is a key verse: "Let them praise Thy Name as great and awful; Holy is He." The Latin version of this verse captures the theme of the psalm perfectly: "*Celebrant nomen tuum magnum et tremendum: sanctum est illud.*"

In my personal reflection on this psalm I was struck by the final paragraph of Mitchell Dahood who says about this psalm: "The seemingly contradictory attributes of the forgiving and punishing God can be reconciled. Even in his grace, Yahweh remains a holy God. This means that he severely punishes the sins of men with the same seriousness of the love by which he forgives sin" (2:370).

Psalm 100

This is designated as a royal psalm or a thanksgiving hymn. This poem is remarkably similar in its expressions to Psalm 95, but has no warnings or negative thoughts within it. It completes a number of the psalms which may be called accession psalms since they were used as one approached the Temple of Jerusalem during a festival. Psalms 93-99 are such psalms. The opening verse is a thanksgiving song which calls upon the nations to join God's people in praise and worship in the Temple.

The structure of the psalm is perfect in simplicity. Verses 1-2 are a call to the worship and service of God. Verses 3-4 give the reason for this praise and worship. Verses 4-5 are a direct call and another reason for the call to worship God. God is the ever faithful Lord who is merciful (*ḥesed*).

The joyful tone of the psalm continues in all of its verses and its exhortation leads the ones praying it to a sense of belonging to God just as a flock belongs to its shepherd. God is central to this hymn and is addressed as Lord (*YHVH*: *Adonai*) five times, and once as God (*Elohim*). Thus God is named six times within five short verses!

We are bathed in an atmosphere of jubilation, pilgrimage, celebration, exaltation and joyful singing. At the conclusion there is a blessing of the holy name of God.

This cheerful psalm is ideal for a short morning prayer since it goes right to the heart of prayer as praise and thanksgiving to God. Its brevity enables me to pray without anxiety, worry, or fret about how to pray. It leaps up at once into prayer that soothes the soul, mind and heart. I think it is a good complement to what some chaplains refer to as the "soldier's night prayer," a term used for a lightning quick prayer on the battlefield. Here it is a time of peace, but offers the weary person a type of "soldier's prayer" in the morning. We need this like some people need to have a cup of coffee to start the day.

Psalm 101

This royal psalm is said by an individual, probably the king of Judah; he says it with a pure and undivided heart. The king is speaking of his ideal plan and dream for ruling over God's people. He also makes it clear that evildoers will not be tolerated in the kingdom.

The structure of the piece is clear and direct. Verses 1-2 show the proper dispositions of the king who directly addresses God in prayer. Verses 3-5 are directed at those who do not comply with the king's desires for integrity, namely, the wicked and the detractors.

132

Verses 6-8 contrast the faithful followers with those who are not righteous.

In reading and praying this psalm, several scriptural passages are helpful. For example, to understand the idealism of the king consider Proverbs 8:15 which reads as follows: "By me kings reign and rulers decree what is just." This reflects the school of wisdom for future rulers of nobility. Another text that helps me is Exodus 34:6: "The Lord passed before him and proclaimed, 'The Lord, the Lord, a God merciful and gracious, slow to anger, and abounding in steadfast love and faithfulness.'" I also found the reference to 2 Samuel 6:9 as helpful: "How can the ark of the Lord come into my care?"

The word "integrity" seemed to capture the sense of the psalm for me. There is a sevenfold pledge on the part of the king which describes his desires to be a man and a ruler with integrity. This comes from his heart which means from his very person. Heart is another key word in this psalm.

We all like integrated people especially if they are called to a public office. Sooner or later most people do acquire a position of authority whether as a parent, teacher, or civil leader. Some of us exercise this on city councils or in the neighborhood gatherings when there are such assemblies.

The psalm fits those who celebrate an anniversary for it provides a healthy format for remembering and thanking God. It serves as a good examination of conscience. All of us seek both interior honesty and wholesomeness. We pray, "O Lord, when will you come to me?"

Psalm 102

This psalm is classified as a lamentation psalm. It has in mind both the individual and the community within its plaint to God. There is also a thanksgiving hymn within the composition. As is my custom, I prefer to keep the psalm as a unit and to remain faithful to the Hebrew tradition. Most scholars assert its unity and there is a tendency to do this more often with other psalms. The canon of the Hebrew Scriptures is to be respected. There are internal indications within the psalm that favor the unity of its composition. One notices a connection through certain repeated words and through the characteristics of Hebrew parallel thought expressed especially in the poetry of the psalms. There is an inclusion within the psalm that also unites its parts.

The structure presented is as follows. Verse 1 is seen as a liturgical superscription which is followed by the lamentation in the Temple by an individual (verses 2-12). There is a transition to a focus on Zion from the one who was lamenting his serious illness. His joy for the sacred city thus gives him a hope for the community and future generations. This is seen in verses 13-23. The final verses (24-28) show the great confidence of the psalmist in the enduring presence of God who is faithful to all generations.

Thus we see a psalm in which the imagery and the rich metaphors describe the sad situation of an individual who appears to be near death. Smoke, indicating the fading of life, burning within one's bones as though they were in a furnace, loneliness like the desert bird (not really a pelican!), or an agitated sparrow on the rooftop, or a moaning owl, shadows which fade as the evening comes on, withering herbage, and worn-out clothes that are changed — all these are used by the poet to express his sad condition. If we remained only with the first part of this psalm, it would almost match Psalm 88 which is the saddest of psalms for a suffering and poor person.

But we turn to Zion and the psalm then becomes quite hopeful and uplifting. The focus of the individual transits into a look at the future with great trust, confidence, and thanksgiving in God's providential care. God is mentioned seven times within the poem (*YHVH*, six times; *Yah*, once). Probably the latter is to be shouted out in praise of God in verse 19.

Within the liturgical setting of this psalm sung within the Temple, the individual becomes concerned with the people of Israel assembled in Zion. Thus the collective identity of Israel is the thrust of the second part of the psalm. We see how an individual who is totally riddled with pain and threatened by death puts all this aside in his love and hope for Zion. Thus there is an eschatological and hopeful perspective coming through because of God's presence within the sacred sanctuary located in Zion (Jerusalem).

I like to remind myself that often I need to see the bigger picture of life, even my life, whenever I reflect or plan things. Personal concerns about health and work are to be seen within the whole of one's life — the bigger picture, as I call it. This reflection like the present psalm helps me overcome self-centeredness, anxiety about the future, and selfishness. Thinking about others and their good example is a big help when I feel down and out. Certainly this psalm resonates within me when I am bothered by doubts, troublesome thoughts, or by total exhaustion. Then, like the psalmist, it is time for me to remember God's presence and God's loving providence. Life then becomes worth living.

Psalm 103

ॐ

This is a magnificent hymn of confidence and praise of God's loving-kindness (*ḥesed*). S. Mowinckel, the renowned Scandinavian scholar of psalms places this psalm among the most religious in experience and originality of thought together with other such psalms of confidence (23, 71 and 73).

The opening verses begin with "Bless the Lord, my soul." This sets the tone for the entire psalm which will end with the blessing of the Lord four times! The poet's heart is totally dedicated to God and God's holy name. The prayer comes from a listening and prayerful heart totally enthralled with the presence of God. The structure of the psalm can be broken into four movements, the first three of which are in praise of God's loving-kindness. Verses 1-5 are the personal praise of an individual who experiences God's forgiveness and loving-kindness which renews his youth like the eagle's. Verses 6-10 harken back to the memory of Moses' time and God's loving-kindness and compassion towards the people of Israel. Verses 11-18 are comprised of striking contrasts of God's mercy and compassion expressed through the heights of heaven with the earth, the distance of east from west, and the loving concern of a father for his children — such is God's loving-kindness in comparison with human weakness and sinfulness. Verses 19-22 are the grand finale which again bless God through the ministry of God's angels and the cosmic choirs. The final verses are an inclusion with the introductory blessing of God.

The psalm demonstrates the religious experience and contemplative nature of the psalmist and his sense of wonder in God's overwhelming compassion and love for creation and for God's people. The primary source for such a religious experience stems from the intimacy that Moses experienced in God's covenant with him and God's people. It is within the context of chapters 33 and 34 of Exodus that some of the expressions of the psalm are rooted (see Exodus 33:13; 34:6; and 34:9).

This psalm is totally focused on God whose name is used twelve times: *YHVH*, eleven times, and "His holy name", once. This, of course, also helps us call to mind the revelation of God to Moses in the burning bush on Mount Sinai. Psalm 19 comes to mind when thinking about the universe and the angelic ministers of God. Uniting with these uses of God's name is the term *hesed* or loving-kindness (see verses 4, 8, 11, and 13). One scholar entitles the psalm "In Praise of *Hesed*" (Schaefer, 253). He notes also that there are 22 verses in the psalm, the number of letters in the Hebrew alphabet thus hinting at a wisdom motif.

Weiser in his work on the psalms captures the prayerful experience of the psalmist in a commentary that in itself is an essay on contemplation and praise. This essay enabled me to go back and enjoy this psalm in prayer and quiet reflection.

My own personal approach in praying the psalms is to do so "with a listening heart." Psalm 103 awakens my heart to the beauty and wonder of God's presence both in the universe and in my heart. I also imagine myself in the Temple of Jerusalem on Mount Zion praying this psalm with the poet. By blessing God, my own heart and spirit listens and beats with the impulse of this contemplative song which I find to be one of my favorites in the Psalter. I know that if prayer becomes a problem for me, this is a psalm I can turn to in order to regain a sense of God's enduring protection and presence. Once again I would then accept God as the center of my life.

Psalm 104

🙐

This magnificent hymn praises the God of all creation. It is grandiose and epic in its scope and serves as an introduction to the next two psalms, 105 and 106, which tell of the salvation history of God among Israel and its inhabitants. This psalm has similar creation themes that are described in Genesis 1 and 2.

A remarkable Egyptian hymn composed by Akhenaton, a heretical pharaoh of the fourteenth century B.C.E., has many of the ideas that are expressed in Psalm 104. In the introduction to the poem in the anthology *Ancient Near Eastern Texts*, we find this description: "The hymn shows the universality and beneficence of the creating and re-creating sun disc" (ANET, 227). More recent commentaries on the psalm say that it stems more from the genius of the psalmist who relies on his own creative skills and his Hebrew traditions about creation for what he expresses in this poem.

My suggested structure for the psalm consists of seven strophes. Verses 1-4: a blessing and praise of God for the creation of light, waters, and wind. Verses 5-9: the creation of the earth, mountains and valleys. Verses 10-18: a continuation of creation seen in vegetation and sentient life in all its variety. Verses 19-23: the marking of the seasons for worship and agriculture through the creation of the moon and the sun. Verses 24-26: a contemplative pause within the psalm praising God's wisdom in creation. Verses 27-30: God's breath brings life to creation; the removal of God's breath takes away life in creatures. Verses 31-35: glory, praise, and honor are given to God. There is a repetition of the opening verse thus forming an inclusion through the word "bless" (*barekh*). Finally, there is a complaint to God to remove those sinners who resist God's beauty in creation.

An eighteenth century scientist, Alexander von Humboldt, had this to say about the psalm: "A single psalm, the 104th, may be said to present a picture of the entire cosmos.... We are astonished to seek within the compass of a poem of such small dimension, the universe, the heavens, with its marvels and beauties, few grand strokes" (Cohen, 237).

The theocentric concentration of this poem is overwhelming. The holy Tetragrammaton for the person of God, the word *YHVH* appears ten times; the word for God (*Elohai*) twice; while the reverential forms of the personal pronoun Thee, Thou, and Thy are used 25 times leaving no doubt that God is blessed, worshiped, and praised constantly throughout this piece because of the wonders of creation. Verse 24, which is like a pause within the psalm, shows the wonder and awe of the poet in contemplating all these works of creation: "How manifold are Thy works, O Lord! In wisdom Thou hast made them all; The earth is full of Thy creatures." Then in verse 31, the poet pauses to praise God again: "May the glory of the Lord endure forever; Let the Lord rejoice in His works."

Recently I read that the eyes of an eight-year-old are open and filled with wonder. I believe that this psalm puts one into that state of amazement through our poet's own contemplation, wonder, and awe in God's creative display through all of the forms of creation. I, too, am astonished how much this psalm moves me to wonder and respect for creation and life in all of its manifestations. We are quite fortunate to have this song extolling God's beauty manifested in the universe and in nature. Like the phrase chosen from Psalm 8 and placed on the moon by the first astronaut, this psalm could easily have been chosen to honor that great giant step in the history of human inventiveness, adventure, and creativity.

Psalm
105
⚘

This psalm is a continuation of the praise of God begun in Psalm 104 which centered on praising God's marvelous creation. Here the theme is salvation history as seen through the miraculous and providential care for Israel, God's chosen people. This is a hymn of thanksgiving for God's constant fidelity seen through the covenant and the prodigies worked for Israel.

Mitchell Dahood states that the psalmist shows great literary artistry in the use of chiastic patterns (seen in verses 15, 22, 43-45) and "explicitation," a technique which emphasizes the last part of a verse as seen in verses 3, 5-6, 17, and 19. There may also be a deliberate wisdom or didactic theme running throughout with verse 23 acting as a swing verse between the first 22 verses of the psalm and the last 22. The Hebrew alphabet has 22 letters within it and usually indicates wisdom and teaching whenever used in the psalms.

For analysis of the structure, I suggest the following divisions for the psalm. Verses 1-6: a preface of praise in which the congregation celebrates the great events in its history. Verses 7-11: God's covenant and the promise of the land of Canaan. Verses 12-15: God's choice and protection of the patriarchs Abraham, Isaac, and Jacob. Verses 16-22: the story of Joseph in Egypt and his leadership and wisdom. Verses 23-24: Jacob and the family are in Egypt. Verses 25-27: the leadership under Moses and Aaron, prophet and priest for the people. Verses 28-38: a description of the plagues upon the Egyptians with plague five and six of the original account in Exodus missing. Verses 39-43: the miracles worked in the desert and in the journey toward the promised land. Verses 44-45: the promised land is entered and the covenant and its relationship to the obedience of Israel are fulfilled.

Psalm 105

This psalm continues the story of Genesis from the call of Abraham to that of Joseph; it then remembers the saving events in the rest of the Torah (Exodus, Leviticus, Numbers, and Deuteronomy). The remembering of the three patriarchs and Joseph is unique to this psalm and is important for understanding their obedience to God, their leadership, and their cooperation with the will of God. All is presented in a liturgical celebration which harkens back to the time when David brought the ark of the covenant to Zion. The psalm, actually presented in 1 Chronicles 16:8-36, parallels what is said in Psalm 105:1-15. History and liturgy are brought together in song as the congregation renews its covenant with God in the Temple. It is especially in the preface that one notices this liturgical jubilation in the use of words like: sing, speak, give thanks, see, seek, rejoice, and look for the face of God (God's presence).

My personal research and reflection on this psalm led me into an appreciation of the ways God providentially led Israel to the promised land. This song is about salvation history which is essential to my own spiritual life. As a believer in God, this trust is enkindled within me upon reading the psalm. It is through the memory of the sacred events that I recall the times when God inspired me or led me through some difficult times. I recall reading a few years ago about a rabbi who taught the congregation about Genesis, but it was only after he had gone through a divorce that the narratives of Genesis really became a part of his life. He then understood its meaning through looking at his own situation in the mystery of God's presence in his life. I am convinced this particular psalm has the power to stir up trust and faith in the God of the covenant who is always guiding us through life. I need to take the time to ponder over the meaning of God in my life and keep searching for and living within God's presence. The narratives of the Torah are filled with practical wisdom for how to live our lives to the fullest.

Psalm
106
᪥

This is the concluding psalm for book four of the Psalter and is a companion to Psalm 105 in that it deals with salvation history but from a liturgical action acknowledging one's sinfulness as a nation. The psalm begins with an introductory liturgy of praise and thanksgiving (verses 1-6) which will be framed with the closing prayer of the whole community of Israel that is gathered in the Temple (verses 47-48). Within these two bookends of the song is the historical poem of national confession of the nation for its infidelities to the great acts accomplished by God that were sung so wondrously in Psalm 105. The psalm has a certain resonance with the books of Exodus and Numbers which narrate the failings and sins of Israel in the desert while the nation wandered forty years. Again and again God's loving-kindness (*hesed*) brings them back. We see the recurring pattern of the Torah: God's covenant is observed, then broken; an act of repentance brings the people back, but once again the cycle of failure begins after the covenant relationship has been restored. God's eternal forgiveness, however, is always experienced once there is an acknowledgment of sinfulness on the part of the people.

A. Weiser associates this psalm with the annual feast of the renewal of the covenant and has found a similar pattern in the *Hodayot* or *Thanksgiving Hymns* found in the Dead Sea Scrolls community at Qumran (circa 135 B.C.E. to 135 C.E.). "The Manual of Discipline prescribes the following: (1) The praise of God in a hymn sung by the priests and Levites followed by the community's response, Amen. Amen. (2) The recital by the priests of the divine saving deeds God has wrought. (3) The recital by the Levites of the 'sins of the Israelites.' (4) The confession of sins of those who enter into the covenant made in recognition of God's righteousness and mercy" (Weiser, 680).

The psalm starts on a positive note with the community preparing itself for the act of forgiveness through its open confession of sin. God's merciful and loving-kindness will be experienced in the sanctuary of the Temple in Zion. God is praised and is beseeched to remember his great merciful acts of salvation so that they may continue in the present. The psalm, in its first five verses, is a beautiful liturgical act of preparation to ask God's pardon for the many times that Israel has forgotten God and the covenant confirmed by the mighty works of the Lord. A question regarding who is worthy to proclaim in full God's praises is asked of the congregation. The answer is confirmed through a beatitude about who is worthy to do this.

Then from verse 7 on, the psalmist in a classical manner recounts in colorful language the seven capital failings of Israel during the Exodus and the ensuing years in the desert even and including failings after the occupation and conquest of the promised land.

Throughout the psalm one can easily find the same failings in the Book of Numbers and in Exodus. Our poet has condensed these events and made them into a sacred remembrance for the community's penitential act. The seven blatant failings are the following:

1. verses 7-12 (Exodus 14:10-14) demonstrates the failure of the Israelites during the crossing of the Red Sea; three different verbs are used for their sin of lacking in faith.
2. verses 13-15 (Numbers 11:4-6) which posits their lusting after the food and fleshpots of Egypt despite God's gift of the manna and quail.
3. verses 16-18 (Numbers 16:25-35) the rebellion of Dathan and Abiram against God's commandments.
4. verses 19-23 (Exodus 32:1-4; Deuteronomy 9:8) the sin of idolatry seen in the making of the molten calf.

143

5. verses 24-27 (Numbers 14:27-29) where the sin of murmuring in the desert against God is recounted.
6. verses 28-31 (Numbers 25:1-9) the fertility rites of the false god Baal are practiced at Peor.
7. verses 32-33 (Numbers 20:10-13) where the Israelites anger God at Meribah and Moses is embittered.

The infidelities are continued even after the conquest of Canaan. Israel has refused to root out all evildoers there; they mingle with the Gentiles and worship their idols (verses 34-39). Even children are sacrificed to the gods of the heathens.

After these atrocious acts of rebellion, idolatry, and even murder of the innocent, the psalm releases the congregation from its guilt. Due punishment has been experienced and now God's ever constant fidelity and loving-kindness are once more enjoyed in the present liturgical action. Verses 44-48 take us back to the opening verses where praise and thanksgiving motifs are expressed. They demonstrate that the people now have their faith in God, who is ever forgiving and merciful, restored. Thus we come full circle in this liturgical psalm of repentance on the part of Israel.

Though we are stunned by the remarkable honesty of the psalmist in describing the grievous sins of the Israelites, we sense the true faith of the people who are praying in the sacred Temple of Zion. They remember all the marvels and wondrous acts of God's love and forgiveness equally with their failings (see verses 1-6, 8-10, 12, 30-31, 44-48). The psalmist who stands for the whole congregation pulls no punches while hanging out their "dirty linen" for all to see/read. They clearly accept the responsibility for their sins. It is all so authentic in offering us a lesson for human growth through the community that acknowledges its failures, surrenders them to God, petitions for salvation, and then praises God's holy name. Hallelujah!

Psalm
107
♀

This psalm is easily seen as the conclusion of a trilogy of psalms starting with Psalm 105. It is broken up in a secondary redaction on the part of the Masoretes (Hebrew scholars from the sixth to the ninth century C.E. who carefully guarded the Hebrew text of the Bible and probably added the superscriptions to the psalms as well as the divisions into five collections) and put as the first psalm for the last or fifth book of the Psalter (Psalms 107-50). The psalm is a communal thanksgiving and hymn which can be broken into two parts, verses 1-31 and 32-43. It is considered by most to be a post-exilic psalm (written after 587 B.C.E.).

The structure is particularly attractive. "Nowhere else in the psalms is there a refrain pattern of comparable intricacy and regularity" (Bullough, 481). This is seen in the use of two antiphonal responses used throughout the first part of the psalm. The antiphons appear for each of the four groups who are being described and who have come to the Temple from all four points of the earth to offer a thanksgiving gift for deliverance from their perils. The description throughout the poem is magnificent, rich, clear and colorful. The use of cognates and of chain-like connectives makes the psalm flow and is pleasant to the ear. The reversals seen in the second part of the psalm are equally striking and lead one to reflect on the loving providence of God (verses 33-43).

The structure for the psalm is clear. Verses 1-3 are the prologue inviting all who have come to Zion from the four quarters of the earth to praise and thank God. This may even be a universal invitation to the nations. Verses 4-32 present the real or ideal trial of four different categories of people called to think about and thank God for their deliverance through the cultic act of thanksgiving in the Temple. They may be pilgrims or wanderers who have come through the desert and are now led in a direct path by God (verses 4-9); or they may be those who have been liberated from dark prisons or from chains (verses 10-16). There are those who have been seriously ill even to the point of falling into the Pit or the deep valleys of death (verses 17-22). Finally, a fourth group are the sea merchants coming from either the west (the Mediterranean Sea) or the south who felt like drunken men tossed here and there, up and down into the depths of the waters (verses 23-32).

In the second part of the psalm, the congregation offers God a hymn in which the reversals of the good and bad in nature and in humans are emphatically proclaimed. This is characteristic of wisdom literature; it is clearly stated in the last verse of the psalm: "Whosoever is wise, let him observe these things, And let them consider the mercies of the Lord" (verse 43). The last two verses are the epilogue, balancing the prologue of the poem. The congregation is called upon to sing the mercies of the Lord who has provided loving care throughout the history of Israel.

This particular psalm was an exhilarating experience for me as I read and prayed it. It offered me hope for all the different types of perils or difficulties I may have experienced in my life. Sometimes I easily lose focus and forget the providence of God. I wander aimlessly in the desert of my mind thinking useless or worrisome thoughts. At other times I am discouraged and may even suffer a slight depression. This happens during the night upon awakening. I am unable to return to sleep because of my thinking about what I have to do or face. This is the dark dungeon suggested in the psalm. Sickness or even the common cold can throw me off and make me short-tempered or irritable. Sickness prevents us from accomplishing anything; even prayer is very difficult. Finally, the ups and downs of my life are similar to the storms at sea that are so graphically described in the psalm. In thinking about these storms, I was amazed at a citation from Joseph Addison found in the *Specta-tor*: "As I have made several voyages upon the sea, I have often been tossed in storms, and on those occasions have frequently reflected on the descriptions of them in different poems. I prefer the following description of a ship in a storm, which the psalmist has made, before any other I have ever met with" (Cohen, 361).

I am led to reflect similarly on my personal experiences which recall the framework of this psalm. If I, like the faithful Israelite, come to the sacred place where God is then I will understand both the epilogue and the conclusion of this wonderful psalm. My heart then is open and listening to the wisdom of God. I am led to appreciate God's love in all of the circumstances of life. Life then becomes worth living.

Psalm 108

This psalm is considered as a compilation of Psalm 57:8-12 for verses 1-6, then from Psalm 60:7-14 for verses 7-14. It is classified as a hymn of individual confidence combined with an individual lamentation in the second part. Dahood is reluctant to take away from its uniqueness and states that it may originate from ancient religious poems. Certainly, the psalmist creatively combines both parts of his poem in its message. The parts are complementary with elements characteristic for a cultic celebration in hymn form. There seems to be a special putting together of the hymn for worship of God for those who have returned from exile. In my estimation, the piece has for its purpose and message to thank God for Israel's deliverance and to call upon God's help now with great confidence for a restoration of the lands promised formerly by God to Israel. The psalmist as an individual speaks for the people while rendering thanks to God and awaiting a manifestation of God's loving-kindness and providential care. Perhaps, a theophany is hoped for in the sacred gathering. The psalm is attributed to David and this, too, recalls the former "good times" that the people experienced under his leadership as their king.

I found the structure suggested in the *New Jerome Biblical Commentary* to be helpful while reading or praying this psalm. Verses 2-5 are a petition. Verses 6-7 are a prayer for deliverance and a divine oracle. Verses 8-14 are a continuation of a prayer for deliverance with an expression of trust (545).

A recent experience I had, similar to what you experience, is a theme from an opera which gets in my mind and memory and stays with me the whole day. This happened to be from a beautiful Italian melody. Earlier that morning I also experienced a sacred piece of music similar to that used for singing the psalms. The two would come over me at different times during the day. Rather than ignoring them, I enjoyed their differences and their hauntingly delightful chords of music. They were there to stay. I think this psalm has such a combination of hymns that resonate well with each other. Like my common experience of a tune within my mind and heart, this psalm was creatively put together by one who was concerned about bringing a joyful and restored hope to the people of Israel.

*Psalm
109*
♋

This psalm is the complaint of an individual. It also has been called a ritual cursing psalm because it contains the longest listing of curses in a psalm (verses 6-20). Because of the harsh imprecations many readers have difficulty with this piece. The interpreters wrestle with it and there are three strains of interpretation offered. The first is to regard the total psalm as the expression of the psalmist's complaints from the beginning to the end. A second creative insight is offered by the translation done in the New Revised Standard Version where the imprecations are those of the oppressors and the unjust who have foisted these curses upon the psalmist. The lengthy section mentioned above is put in quotation marks indicating that it belongs to the ruthless speech of the wrongdoers who are presenting their unjust case in a court. The change from the singular (the psalmist) to the plural (the wrongdoers) give legitimacy to such an interpretation. We realize there are no punctuation marks in the original text and therefore even punctuation is a form of interpretation. That leads us to a third possibility for understanding the psalm. I found two scholars, Konrad Schaefer and Sebastian Bullough, offering us a unique way of looking at this psalm and others that have curses within them. They see the curses all belonging to the genre of hyperbole used in Deuteronomy in contrasting blessings with curses. This is a help to put us in the frame of mind that goes back into biblical times. Bullough, whom I find saying something similar to Schaefer cites C.S. Lewis, the famous literary theologian who in *Reflections on the Psalms* says, "The absence of anger, especially that sort of anger which we call *indignation*, can, in my opinion, be a most alarming symptom (30), suggesting a 'terrifying insensibility' and a 'total moral indifference'" (Bullough, 482). Schaefer sends us back to Deuteronomy 27:15-

WITH A LISTENING HEART

26 and 28:15-46, the scriptural source for curses as opposed to blessings. While reading this psalm in the light of Deuteronomy and realizing that it is set in an atmosphere similar to a court-room with an adversary offering the curses from the wicked ones, enables the reader to see that God will ultimately be the just advocate and the judge in such unjust proceedings on the part of aggressive evildoers.

Combining Schaefer's insight with his revised structure of the NRSV we have the following for the psalm's verses. (1) Verses 1-5 are an appeal from the psalmist to God for help. (2) Verses 6-20 are the ritual curses of the psalmist directed against the unjust. (3) Verses 21-29 are the poet's request for just ret-ribution with his own vindication present. (4) Verses 30-31 are the conclusion which match the beginning of the psalm. There is also a sense that, through the praise and thanksgiving in-ferred, the psalmist has found what he was looking for in the courtroom of life's unsavory experiences.

I know that most of us experience some form of cursing foisted on us by others through their misunderstanding of our motives, or through false opinions, or through cruel remarks against us. No matter what we say or do, it is judged to be wrong by certain people. They simply do not like us and make it known in some strong statements that cut through to our deepest self. Avoidance, calumny, false judgments are other forms that act like curses against us. Most of us are sensitive and feel hurt when any of these "curses" happen to us. I was personally helped by what C.S. Lewis wrote about "The Cursings" in chapter 3 of *Reflections on the Psalms*. Perhaps, with such suggestions, the psalm may be read and even prayed. It could also be a way of legitimately working through our angry feelings about those who have hurt us. Some of our pent-up anger may be justified and some of it not. It is worthwhile bringing these feelings into the psalm as we attempt to read or pray it. It is worth a try.

Psalm
110

❦

This is one of the most beautiful of the royal messianic psalms. It may be from the time of Solomon's reign (961-922 B.C.E.). It was composed to celebrate the coronation of a king in Zion who was a descendant of David. It is closely related to the idealism expressed in Psalm 2, but issues at a time when the warrior king is being extolled and praised after a victory.

Both Judaism and Christianity have seen messianic royalism in this psalm; however, in the tradition of the Christians this psalm takes on a Christological messianic interpretation and is applied to Jesus of Nazareth. It is cited in all four gospels and a total of 25 times within the Christian Scriptures (New Testament), thus being the most cited of the Hebrew texts.

I have structured the psalm according to the two prophetic oracles that are found within it at the beginning in verses 1-3, and then a new oracle in verses 4-7. The oracle is presented with a formula that is the prophetic word of God; thus it has great revelatory significance. We notice that these oracles speak of both the king and the priest probably combined in the same Davidic ruler. In the Dead Sea Scrolls there is mention of two messiahs: one is a king, the other a priest. Christians blend both king and priest into the kingship of Jesus which is eschatological or beyond this world.

The psalm presents God as the supreme ruler over this king-priest figure. The psalm thus has a pre-exilic tone about it by totally centering on the theocracy of God as king with the earthly ruler as a vice-regent. The Hebrew tradition associates the psalm with David before the Temple is built, after the bringing of the ark of the covenant to Zion, and David is standing to the right vested in royal priestly robes. He has just come from a great victory and the people are invited to celebrate him as king. A prophet or priest announces his glorious presence within the oracular prophecy mentioned above. Throughout the verses it is God's kingship and God's holiness that is central.

The word pictures in this psalm are exceptionally striking. The messiah king places his feet over the heads of the conquered Gentile rulers (verse 1). In the oracle God extends the scepter over the king and God is at the right hand of the king as warrior whenever the need to battle for Israel arises (verses 2 and 5). The fascinating text refers to the priestly and kingly order of Melchizedek who has no beginning and no end, no apparent origin. There may be an eschatological significance here in a text that is based on Genesis 14:18 where Melchizedek is described as king of Salem and priest of God Most High (*El Elyon*). The final verse of the psalm images the king as drinking from a brook after the victory or drinking from a special fount, perhaps, from Zion's water source.

In today's society we are not prone to praise kings or priests in this manner. Too many misuses of political power and military power come to our minds, and the recent scandals of abuse among priests who have broken the great trust that was given to them crush our spirits. Returning to the psalm we discover that the centrality of God has often been missed by both priests and kings (political persons who have authority). The wisdom of seeing the bigger picture is lacking in them and they fall far short of being models for our youth. On our own level we are called to be integrated in our dealings with one another and never to betray a trust in a relationship. Our gifts of mind and heart are precious and yet fragile. They are to be developed carefully for the common good and our well-being. We may not have an oracle or prophetical announcement about this but we do have the Scriptures and the psalms, especially this one, to reflect upon.

Psalm
111
ॐ

This is a beautiful hymn which is called an alphabetical psalm. The composer or Temple
musician used the 22 letters of the Hebrew alphabet to structure the poem that involves the
chanter and the congregation. I consider the
alphabet as the preferred structure of the author and therefore will not break this psalm
into verses or divisions. It is best to allow the
psalm to speak for itself through the literary technique of an
acrostic reading of the poem.

This Levite or choirmaster opens his heart to thank God.
His thought is closely allied with the perspective I had when
thinking of this book which I call, "With a Listening *Heart*."
The Hebrew has a double use of the word heart thus intensify-
ing its activity in the person who prays or sings the psalm: "Hebrew 'with a whole heart,' with a heart completely absorbed in
the duty to offer Him praise" (Cohen, 374).

The psalm is a recital of the great and mighty acts of God
on behalf of Israel, God's people. In it we easily become aware
of the four pillars of the recital and of today's Judaism: the love
of God, the reverence for the Torah, the people or elect nation
of God, the land. In the psalm the Exodus and the miracles connected with it are recalled (*zakhar*). There is a remembrance
that makes these saving acts come alive today for the one praying. The psalm takes place in a liturgical celebration that involves the people in a renewal of the covenant they have made
with God. The word for covenant appears twice and the fact
that it is eternal is expressed four times within this poem (verses
5, 8, 9, 10). Both the individual and the community are involved
in recital of God's saving acts. The love of God streams through
each letter of the alphabet and what follows (usually just three
or four words). We read of God's covenant attributes: glory,
majesty, graciousness, justice, loving-kindness, compassion

and divine providence. In the final verse we are led to embrace biblical wisdom which is the reverence or awe that we have in the presence of God. It is caught in the proverbial phrase, "The fear of the Lord is the beginning of wisdom" (verse 10). Like the covenant, God's praise endures forever.

I admire the inventiveness of the psalmist who created this marvelous prayer and poem. By using the alphabet, we are led to consider the basics of our relationship to God. By taking one letter at a time, we are able to slow down and ponder over and realize the sacredness of the present moment of prayer and contact with the holy name of God. We take one step at a time. We come to realize that God is praised through each letter of the alphabet and that the whole Psalter depends upon the use of the alphabet in each word and verse. We take time to smell the roses and to tiptoe through God's garden, the Psalter.

Psalm 112

This is a wisdom psalm similar to Psalms 1, 19, and 119. At once it is easily seen as the twin to Psalm 111 which is an acrostic of ten lines just as is Psalm 112. The very last verse of the former psalm is a wisdom saying which leads into the opening verse of our present psalm. Both psalms have as the invitatory verse the invocation "Praise the Lord" (Hallelujah). We discover immediately that the fear of the Lord is used seven times within these psalms thus indicating that true wisdom consists in a reverential and loving respect for God which is termed fear of the Lord. Wisdom consists in observing the commandments and precepts of God with joy and ease. We notice that nine of the ten verses show how this is done; only verse ten brings in the strong Semitic flavor for contrasting the wicked and their downfall with the righteous and wise person.

Psalm 1 immediately comes to mind where the righteous is contrasted with the wicked in the parallelism of each thought in Psalm 1; in our present psalm the virtues of the wise are seen in every verse except the last. It is due to the alphabetical structure of the psalm that a great number of repetitious praises are applied to the wise person. The wicked are squeezed into verse 10 with colorful description as to their failure and defeat into oblivion.

Scholars are almost unanimous in considering Psalms 111 and 112 as having the same structure, content, and vocabulary in certain verses. The first psalm emphasized the praise of God's attributes while the present psalm sees these attributes as embraced by the wise and righteous. These are the ones who carry out God's commands after having reflected upon God's works in Psalm 111.

Wisdom literature, especially in the opening lines of Proverbs and also in the second and third parts, emphasizes this wondrous reverential fear of the Lord. Readers should take note that this is a healthy attitude of wonder and respect, not a negative feeling of anxiety or terror before the presence of God. The virtues of the holy and wise who observe God's laws bring them great delight. Their hearts are steadfast and trusting in the Lord. Virtues are relational and build up friendships both with other people and certainly with God. Generosity towards others is seen in this psalm (verse 9). The wise and righteous are perpetually happy people.

I sense that the one who composed this psalm had a close relationship with God. The mercy, compassion, and justice are attributes of the Almighty and yet this psalmist shared in them and extended them to the listening congregation possibly during the time of Zechariah and Haggai when the Temple was being rebuilt. There is much to learn from this didactic poem teaching us the ABCs of life.

In a recent Christian and Jewish dialogue I heard Lorraine, one of the Jewish members speaking about *Shavuot* (Feast of Weeks and of the Harvest). She mentioned the *Tiqqun Leyl Shavuot* which is an all-night stay in the synagogue while studying the Torah. She made it up until 3:30 in the morning and then decided to go home instead of falling asleep where she was praying and studying. She was practicing what our psalm speaks of, namely, wisdom. The psalm helps faithful people observe God's *mitzvoth* (good acts of kindness to others because of the teachings of the Torah); this makes the world a better place to live in. The world is on its true course when we all are living the commandments of God and are fitting into God's eternal plan of wisdom. *Tiqqun 'Olam*, the way the world should move, is then being accomplished.

Psalm 113 ☙

This psalm is a beautiful and consoling hymn. It initiates the Hallel psalms (113-18) with the characteristic summons, "Hallelujah"... praising the Lord. This series of psalms is recited during the great pilgrimage festivals of *Pesah*, *Shavuot*, and *Sukkot* (Passover, Feast of Weeks, and the Feast of Tabernacles). These psalms are also used for the dedication of the Temple and the new moon festivals in honor of God the Creator. In the familial setting of the Passover, Psalms 113-14 are recited before the meal; Psalms 115-18 after the meal.

The psalm is structured in three strophes in the Hebrew. Verses 1-3: Hallelujah! This is the summons for the congrega-

156

tion to praise God through God's Name. Verses 4-6: God is seen as transcendent and majestic; therefore, God is praised. Verses 7-9: The loving concern of God is lavished upon the poor, the needy, and the barren. Here we see the immanence or the horizontal dimension of God's presence among us.

The Hebrew word *Shem* means Name and is the reverent and pious way of proclaiming God's nature which was revealed to Moses through the miracle of the burning bush (Exodus 3:14). The Torah is the great source for God's revelation of who God is (cf. verse 6). God's praise extends through every epoch in human history and in every space in nature. God is praised thus in time and space in this psalm. The rhetorical question of "Who is like unto the Lord?" is, in my opinion, the central reason for this hymn of praise. God is the totally Other, the *Mysterium tremendum*, the All Holy One who is and causes creation. As the Creator, God looks down upon the heavens and the earth. In fact, the Hebrew has the colorful notion of God stooping down to peer upon creation.

The final three verses are the comforting reality of God's concern for the *'anavim* (the poor), the needy and the barren woman. Thus the lowliest person is loved by God. Those who need God most are cared for and consoled by God alone. Here the psalm shows the immanence of God in the protection of Zion and the people of Israel who are the congregation singing this psalm in the restored Temple.

The following interpretation is right at the heart of this psalm in verse 6: "that looketh down low," literally "who cometh down low to look." "Transcendence is only one aspect of God's nature; it does not preclude his concern about the welfare of his creatures. An attribute of great importance for the theological conception of God, one upon which both biblical and rabbinical literature laid especial stress, is his condescension and humility.... This truth has a religious depth which no philosophy can set forth. Only the God of revelation is near to man in his frailty and need, ready to hear his sighs, answer his supplication, count his tears, and relieve his wants when his own power fails" (Cohen, 379).

This psalm made me recall my first year of studying Hebrew with an outstanding linguist, Brother Gerard Sullivan, S.M. It was almost fifty years ago and three of us were under Brother's tutelage. He had us memorize this psalm and all three of us then repeated it to him. The most intelligent among the three was named by Brother as Ben Yehudah; the next most brilliant, Yohanan; and I was given the name Menaḥem (the consoler). Well, Yehudah received an "A", Yohanan a "B", and I, Menaḥem, received a "C"! Since I had a competitive streak in me, I studied under Rabbi Ira Sud in Chester, Pennsylvania the next year. At the end of the Hebrew course with Brother Sullivan, Yehudah received an "A", Yohanan a "B", and Menaḥem a "B"! No wonder I was called the consoler!

Psalm 114

This great poetic hymn celebrates the miracles of Exodus. The psalm is beautifully structured using both Hebrew parallelism of the synonymous type, colorful descriptions of God's theophany in the Exodus and Sinai events, and balance in the four strophes in this quality piece. A. Weiser in his commentary on the psalms offers one of the best essays on Psalm 114. His theological insights, spiritual sensitivity, and exegetical ability shine through and let the reader appreciate what this psalm is all about (708-13). I am indebted to him for many of the comments I make about this psalm and have used his structural analysis for the poem. It consists of the

following four strophes. First strophe (verses 1-2): The miracles
of the Exodus event and the birth of a nation, Israel. Second
strophe (verses 3-4): The crossing of the Red Sea, and the River
Jordan being turned back. Third strophe (verses 5-6): Wonder
and appreciation for the works of God in the miracles of Exodus. Fourth strophe (verses 7-8): The response to the poet's
questions. We see in this psalm the cornerstone of the people
of Israel bound up with the names of Jacob, Judah, and Israel
the people chosen and elected by God who is their real king. We
see that all of the salvific acts of Exodus are rendered as present
in the assembly where both a covenant ceremony and a worship
service take place celebrating the freedom and liberation the
people now enjoy from an alien tongue of a barbaric people.
There is in the remembering of these events of God an actual-
izing of them that takes on a special quality of reenacting them
today. God is saving and protecting Israel today as this psalm
is said in the Temple. God is king of the universe and of the
chosen people of Israel.

The miracles of nature are quite colorfully described in an
impressive way in the crossing of the Red Sea and the rolling
back of the River Jordan. The poetic talent of the psalmist is
especially seen in the strophes in which the miracles are compared to rams and sheep leaping and bounding over the mountains and hills. Israel no longer hears the barbarous language of
the foreign oppressor. Now the people are free to sing in their
own tongue in a sacred space on Mount Zion. True freedom is
experienced in the promised land.

The description is playful, colorful, and wonderful. It is
filled with chiastic word order, merisms, and parallels in the
thought and imagery — all harmoniously blended in their effectiveness. The lines jump out and sing for the one who listens or reads them. God's wondrous actions are celebrated with
ecstatic joy. This short poem is one of the most beautifully con-

structed in the Psalter. It is not only beautiful as a psalm, it is also theological in understanding how God works out salvation history for Israel. The theme expressed by the words "going out" (*yaẓa*) is at the heart of the theology of Exodus. The theophany speaks to us of the giving of the Torah on Sinai. Creation out of chaos is seen in the symbolism of the water verses where liberation is achieved, pools emanate for the thirsting people, and rocks pour out fresh water. The whole psalm is uplifting for the congregation and gives them a sense of hope for the future because God is ever present to them throughout this psalm.

In my heart's reflection on the poem and its meaning for me today, I am led to appreciate my own family origins, my religion and spirituality, and my being part of a blessed nation. A sense of wonder floods over me when I remember the saving acts of God in my life as a member of a community of believers and as an individual. By remembering the significant good happenings in my life, the sacred experiences of prayer and friendships, I too have a sense of hope. Psalm 114 is a source for these memorable events in life. I can appreciate the words of the poet who composed this not only as a piece of literature but also as a prayer for a listening heart.

Psalm 115

☙

This combines both lamentation with a hymn praising the glory of God. It is best to consider this psalm as separate from Psalm 114, whereas the Septuagint and the Vulgate join them. The antiphonal nature of the song and its alternation with a cantor and the congregation are evident in the structure and the change of the personal pronouns.

The psalm is difficult to date. Dahood sees some pre-exilic features in it; others because of its language see it as post-exilic or even exilic because of similarities with Deutero-Isaiah and Jeremiah. There is no doubt, however, that it is celebrated in a liturgy that extols God the benevolent Creator who is to be glorified. Perhaps, the congregation is hoping that God will manifest this divine glory to the humiliation of the Gentiles.

The lamentation springs from the taunts and humiliating remarks about Israel's belief in *YHVH*. The priest or cantor stirs up the trust and confidence of the people to extol God's glory while trusting that the divine glory will appear in their liturgical celebration.

The structure of the psalm consists of three strophes with four verses each and then a final strophe that has three verses. The Hebrew interpretation sees verses 1-8 as the song of the Levite, whereas 9-15 is the response of the congregation, while the last lines are the blessings to be hoped for through the priestly prayer offered.

The psalm thus starts with its lamentation but quickly extols the covenantal attributes of God's glory, mercy and truth (*ḥesed, emet*). The presence of God is sensed throughout the whole poem; God in one form or the other of God's name is mentioned 14 times and even once more in the concluding "Hallelujah" (Praise ye *Yah*). God is the only Holy One who can vindicate divine glory by humiliating the nations who have humbled and ridiculed the people of Israel, God's glory here on earth. The vindication of God would bring an end to the mockery of the Gentiles at the expense of God's elect.

In verses 4 through 8, our psalm gives a powerful and sarcastic rebuttal of the taunts of the Gentiles. Their gods are human artifacts. Seven times the poet and congregation hold these lifeless images in derision. Every one of the five senses are lacking in the idols; all is ornamental, sham, and impotent ("All that glitters is not gold")!

Ibn Ezra captures the spirit of the psalm saying "may they that make them be like them... men make gods after their own image, and when made the gods make them after theirs" (see Cohen, 384).

From verse 9 the confident response of the choir or congregation is heard and God's glory as Creator is extolled. The house of Israel, the house of Aaron, and those who truly fear God participate in the response on three successive refrains. This is probably the entire believing congregation of Israel and not proselytes. Our hymn is highly centered on the nation of Israel and on the theocentrism of its celebration in the liturgy. The blessings obtained from God are apparent in both the old and the young and all who are fully alive with belief in *YHVH*; outside of Israel there is only the foolish belief of the Gentiles who are the makers of their own gods. The dead cannot praise God nor experience the glory and wonder of the God of Israel.

Paraphrasing the Talmud we see that humans should occupy themselves with God's glory as revealed in the Torah and God's salvific marvels and benevolent acts. These are to be appreciated and celebrated while we are fully alive, for in death we can no longer do this, and God, the Holy One, blessed be He, finds naught to praise in the dead.... The thought of being consigned to the lower regions called Sheol (Hades) arouse in the Hebrew a feeling of horror and dismay; but the righteous are upheld by the belief that their stay would not be eternal. God would not leave them in Sheol, but bring them up again to enjoy His Presence (Cohen, 384 and 14).

In participating in a good number of Jewish burials and listening to the eulogies and the passages chosen from the *Tanakh*, I sensed that the spirit of this psalm is quite alive among those who attend. There is a hope and a trust in the absolute goodness of the Creator that continues life both in one's children, one's good deeds and words, and also in the mystery of death which is another marker in one's relationship with God.

Psalm 116

An individual psalm of thanksgiving. Though the Septuagint (250 B.C.E.) and the Vulgate (405 C.E.) break the text into Psalms 114 and 115, the Masoretic text presents Psalm 116 as a whole. The Masoretes are the ones who have handed down the official living tradition of the text (from 500-900 C.E.) and this is the current presentation of the psalm. I follow it in general throughout this work on the psalms.

The first line presents a problem for the commentators who see that God is the one who takes the initiative in love. I have followed the observation of M. Dahood on this point and likewise have adapted his structural presentation of the psalm here. His translation for the first verse is: "Out of love for me Yahweh did hear my plea for his mercy." This makes sense for it is God who answers the prayer of the psalmist and God who loves and inclines a listening ear to the person in need. The poet does cry out in verse 4 and asks to be delivered from what he has described as life-threatening sickness. God's healing power (seen in calling upon the name of God) is invoked. Dahood rightly observes that an "accusative of cause" followed by the objective first person singular shows that God is the doer both in love and mercy towards the poor one crying out in God's name. This results in the offering of a thanksgiving libation and a fulfilled promise on the part of the one who has new life. All this is taking place in the Temple in Jerusalem.

The magnanimous divine qualities of God's covenant are recalled in verse five: God's graciousness, justice, and mercy. The person who prays devoutly (one of the "poor of *YHVH*" or an *'anavim*) is answered because of the absolute trust and dependence offered in this poem. This sentiment perdures throughout the psalm making this a perfect form of prayer and for imaging God in such a magnificent way. These comments complete the first six verses of the psalm which are sung before the congregation gathered in the Temple. Later this psalm would be used for the Passover celebration.

Verses 7-11 are the prayer and reflections of the psalmist or the one praying this psalm. The poet is thankful to God for the deliverance from death and from recovering from his illness. In this respect several commentators remark the similarity to Hezekiah's miraculous recovery from a serious illness (see Isaiah 38:9-20).

In verse 11 a corrective is suggested which normally reads "all men are liars." "Rather, the whole of man is deceptive; his power to assist is unreliable (cf. vain is the help of man, Psalm 60:13). The noun from this root occurs in 62:10, *men of low degree are vanity, and men of high degree are a lie*" (Cohen, 386).

Verses 12-15 are words addressed to the assembly on the part of the psalmist or the Levite chanting this section in the Temple. How can anyone ever repay God for such love, goodness, and mercy? A thanksgiving offering is admittedly a meager way of doing this on the part of the psalmist. But it is done with openhearted sincerity and devotion and is acceptable to

God. The libation could be shared as well as poured around the altar by the Levites thus intimating the thanksgiving for being healed.

Verses 16-18 are the response in song coming from the congregation which joins the faithful poet in the thanksgiving to God. The identification of the psalmist as one of the "poor of *YHVH*" is evident in verse 16 while the other three verses make clear the whole purpose of the psalm.

This is one of my favorite psalms because of its personal sentiments and because it connects with me as a believer who loves the liturgy. My entire being is drawn by the words which seem to be so close to the way I like to thank God. The psalm has been used both in the Jewish liturgy and in the liturgy of the Catholic Church surrounding the Eucharist. Thus in both Jewish and Christian worship services it is an excellent response of thanksgiving to God who heals us of all our infirmities both of mind and body. This psalm would be a good one for us to offer on Thanksgiving Day.

Psalm 117

This is the shortest psalm in the Psalter and is classified as a hymn. It is one of the Egyptian Hallel psalms (113-18). The structure is clear. Verse 1 is a call to praise and worship God. Verse 2 is the reason why all nations and peoples should worship God. The Hebrew usually indicates such a reason by the conjunctive word *ki* which is usually translated as "because" or "for." It is the assembly of God that is summoned in this psalm, but its content is universal, a theme found throughout the Hebrew Bible or *Tanakh*. This universal call is God's revelation. God is ever steadfast in divine love (*hesed*) and God's fidelity to promises is eternal (*emet*). In the Christian Scriptures St. Paul of Tarsus uses this psalm to include the Gentiles and he is known as the apostle to the Gentiles thus testifying to the universalism of the psalm (see Romans 15:11). The attributes of God mentioned are those that are shown to humankind and are the reason for rendering praise to God through Israel.

I found it interesting that Countess Mary Sidney of Pembroke (ca. 1561-1621) took this short poem and fashioned it into an acrostic reading thus spelling out the meaning of the psalm. She found it to be a true Hallel psalm in that it does praise God with a Hallelujah. Here is her beautiful rendition:

> Praise him that aye
> Remains the same:
> All tongues display
> Jehovah's fame.
> Sing, all that share
> This earthly ball:
> His mercies are
> Exposed to all:
> Like as the word
> Once he doth give,
> Roll'd in record,
> Doth time outlive.

B.W. Fisken writes of Mary Sidney's "insistence on the validity of applying to the psalms knowledge and understanding gained from study and personal experience that makes them models for private meditation" (cited in Holladay, 207-08). In a sense, this is the whole purpose of my sharing the reflections at the end of each psalm. This is what I mean to "have a listening heart" or *lev shome'a*.

166

Psalm 118

🜍

This psalm is considered a community thanksgiving, a hymn of praise and thanksgiving and a royal victory hymn. Upon reading it carefully, one sees that the psalm contains all of these qualities. The themes are active and dynamic because they are set within a great liturgical celebration that includes a procession, an entrance ritual into the gates of righteousness, and cultic symbols that fit the processional festivities of one of the great pilgrimage feasts, *Sukkot,* or the harvest feast of booths. In most celebrations of pilgrimage the themes of the Exodus are recalled (here the Song of Moses and of Miriam in Exodus 15). The presence of the king as leader also suggests an enthronement of Yahweh theme within the scope of this marvelous psalm. The king, who represents the great figure of King David, is at the center of this psalm (verses 5-19) and is the one who leads the congregation in procession. Upon approaching he sings out to the priests who are to open the gate of Righteousness for Israel, for the other priests and Levites, and for the ones who have come from other nations, the godfearers or proselytes. The ritual of entering is reminiscent of Psalm 24.

For the structure of the psalm, the following is suggested. Verses 1-4: An invocation of Israel, of the House of Aaron, and of those who fear the Lord is sung by the congregation gathered outside the gates of the Temple. Verses 5-18: The king prays and sings individually a victorious hymn of triumph over the enemies of Israel. Verses 19-25: The procession of people desirous to enter the gates of the Temple take up the antiphonal responses so repetitive in this psalm. Verses 26-29: The cultic acts of thanksgiving are now offered around the altar in the sanctuary of the Temple.

The pageantry in this wondrous song of thanksgiving and

celebration is overwhelming with its praise of God (*YHVH* 22 times; *Yah*, 5 times; *El*, 3 times). The song is alternated between the chorus and the congregation; then the carrying of myrtle, palm, and willow branches near and around the altar is suggestive of this festival called *Sukkot*. Dancing enlivens the crowd and brings the procession to a successful conclusion in the Temple on Mount Zion. Joy, exuberance, and song fill the halls.

Within the psalm is the symbolism of the cornerstone which is either the keystone at the top of a gate or arch or the foundation stone joining two sides of the Temple wall. This stone represents God's selection of Israel over the other nations who reject God's choice. Yet, this is the day the Lord has made and Israel rejoices in it. It is an actualization of the experience the people have of God's presence on this festival of booths and of *YHVH*. There may be a subtle hint that the Gentiles are included in the expression of those who fear God or the proselytes from the nations. The psalm ends as it began with a fitting conclusion to the Hallel psalms celebrating Israel's liberation from Egypt.

Perhaps, it is fitting here to recall that Martin Luther cherished this psalm as his favorite. He writes, "This is my psalm which I love — for truly it has deserved well of me many a time and has delivered me from many a sore affliction when neither the emperor nor kings nor the wise nor the cunning nor the saints were able or willing to help me" (Weiser, 723-24).

Sholom Aleichem, the Jewish novelist, has given us a delightful description for the festival of *Sukkot* which captures the spirit of the psalm and the festival: "To me it is the finest time of the year. Each day is a gift from heaven. The sun no longer bakes like an oven but caresses with a heavenly softness. The woods are still green, the pines give out a pungent smell. In my yard stand the *sukke* — the *sukke* I have built for the holiday, covered with branches, and around me the forest looks like a

Psalm 119

huge *sukke* designed for God Himself. Here, I think, God celebrates his holiday, here and not in town, in the noise and tumult" (Glinert, 229). The *sukke* (or *sukkah*) is the temporary booth or tabernacle erected for this festival.

In reading this psalm in the context of the last two citations, I, too, am led into a prayerful experience and a contemplative mode. I am led to sing and dance in the presence of the God of Israel.

Psalm 119

This is the longest psalm in the Psalter, consisting of 176 lines. It is commonly classified as a wisdom psalm, but it contains features of a hymn, lamentation, and thanksgiving. However, it is best to put all of these different types under the label of wisdom, for the psalm focuses on the wisdom of God's precepts and commandments as experienced by those who live them out through the Torah. By taking one stanza at a time, one comes to appreciate this prayer which is constructed upon the letters of the alphabet for each stanza of eight lines. Since there are 22 letters of the alphabet in Hebrew, the psalm results in 176 verses. Throughout the central theme is love and dedication to the Torah of God seen in the commandments, words, and decrees of God. Torah is best understood as the revelation, the instruction, and the teaching of God rather than the law of God which has different connotations for us today. Within the carefully constructed poem there are eight key words which guide us through the psalm. From *Alef* to *Tav* (or A to Z) we discover most of these words in each stanza; those which have all eight may be considered a perfect stanza. It is helpful to look at Psalm 1 and especially at Psalm 19:8-15 for

169

the spirit of Psalm 119 and for the possible source for a number of the key or thematic words.

I offer the following description of what these eight words mean in the context of the psalm. These key words are:

1. *Torah*: best understood as a teaching, direction, and revelation coming from God through Moses. The Torah is often referred to as the first five books of the Hebrew Scriptures, but it is also the living out of God's commands and precepts that are involved in the experience of prayer and righteous living. The term "law" does not contain what Torah is, but it is frequently the translation offered in English.

2. *'edut*: usually translated as testimony or testimonies in the plural. These are the rules of one's conduct seen as attesting to conformity to the will of God. Decalogue, evidence, the ark of the covenant, divine decree, and an open acknowledgment of God's way are part of the meaning contained in this word.

3. *Piqqudim*: the precepts or personal rules to be obeyed or carried out in the principles of a righteous life before God.

4. *Huqqim*: the engraved laws or statutes that govern the more public life of Israel. The directives for community living are implied in this word.

5. *Mizvah* or *Mizvot*: the laws of God as lived out in good deeds. They are characteristic of good, religious living out of the principles of the Torah with joy. The word especially concerns deeds done for another person.

6. *Mishpat*: principles and rules of conduct in relationship to our neighbor. Often the word is translated as judgment or decree.

7. *Davar*: means "word" but in the sense of a reality that is expressive of God's will.

8. *Imrah*: a poetic expression similar to the word *davar* but more in keeping with the promises of God expressed in sayings.

170

Psalm 119

The structure of this psalm is seen through the use of an acrostic wherein each letter of the alphabet is used for a stanza of eight lines while at the same time being used for each line under the given stanza. Thus A or the first stanza starts with an *Alef* in Hebrew for each of the eight verses and so on till the last letter of the alphabet, the *Tav*, is completed.

I see the content of the psalm consisting of the eight key words which are woven throughout the stanzas. Within the stanzas are also found the emotions, motivations, apprehensions, and moods of the psalmist. This makes the psalm an excellent personal and intimate prayer. In reflecting upon the whole of the psalm, I think that Psalm 19:14 may have been the source of its inspiration: "Let the words of my mouth and the meditation of my heart be acceptable to you, O Lord, my rock and my redeemer."

I now have tried to put in a succinct way the meaning of the 22 stanzas:

Alef (1): Happy and blessed are they who live out, study, and observe Torah (see Psalm 1).

Bet (2): Your Torah, O Lord, brings delight to my heart and soul.

Gimel (3): Give me the gift of your Torah, O Lord, even in the midst of my struggles with oppressors of your decrees.

Dalet (4): O Lord, I am oppressed with sorrow, I beseech you to teach and console me.

Hé (5): Enliven me, O Lord, and make light for your paths that I may follow your teachings faithfully.

Vav (6): With your assistance, O Lord, I am joyful of professing your truth even before the powerful ones. "The pleasure which accompanied the performance of God's commands is a theme upon which the rabbis expatiated. According to them, 'this joy of the mitzvah (commandment) constituted the essence of the action'" (Cohen, 399).

Zayin (7): In the psalmist's affliction and sorrow the Torah is his solace and joy. The word Torah appears three times in this stanza and the Lord quickens or gives life to the poet. This life-giving experience is mentioned nine times within the psalm.

Het (8): The poet is totally committed to keeping the Torah and its precepts; he is a friend to the righteous but detests the lawless or unrighteous. This is a perfect stanza which has all eight of the key words.

Tet (9): The psalmist asks the Lord to teach him how to observe the commandments during a time of affliction. There is an unusual twist to this petition for discernment and for understanding his sufferings and afflictions.

Yod (10): The psalmist asks the Lord to approve of him and to console him in his sufferings, whereas the Lord should confound the impious and lawless. This verse contains all of the eight key words and may be termed a "perfect" stanza.

Kaf (11): Another perfect stanza in which the poet implores the Lord to help him. His oppressors are probably the leaders in the community, by whom he is sorely tried.

Lamed (12): The Lord's word (*davar*) is stable, limitless, delightful, and inexhaustible in its perfection.

Mem (13): The poet says, "How I loved Thy Torah." This is the central theme of the psalm. In my reflection upon this, I see the introductory Psalm 1 being lived out through this theme which is meditated upon throughout the day, seven times. Seven of the key words are used in this stanza.

Nun (14): The Torah is light for the psalmist which leads him through the darkness of oppression and suffering.

Samekh (15): He is pure of heart or single-minded when it comes to observing Torah; the double-minded are abominable to him. The word of the Lord is a shield and a refuge.

'Ayin (16): Since he is faithful to the Torah, the psalmist

now asks for help against his oppressors. In verse 122 of this stanza there is no key word used, a rarity in this psalm.

Pé (17): Lord, instruct and protect me for I admire and love your Torah. The stanza is perfect in using all eight key words. A powerful image is given of the stream of tears which overwhelm him as he mourns the lack of observance of God's commandments (verse 136).

Zadé (18): Lord, your Torah is justice; it endures forever and is pure. The psalmist is zealous for all of God's precepts.

Qof (19): The psalmist almost cries out in prayer, "Lord, grant me the grace of living according to your Torah!" He is vigilant during the dark hours before dawn; he prays.

Resh (20): The prayer here is, "O Lord, save me from my persecutors and from liars, for truth is at the heart of your word and your decrees are eternal" (verse 160).

Shin (21): The Torah fills the psalmist with joy, reverence, peace, love, and confidence.

Tav (22): The image of a lost and wandering sheep is used to describe the poet. He begs the Lord to hear his cry and to free him and teach him the way of the commandments.

Because of the great length of this psalm many are not fond of it, but by way of my own working through such a problem, I discovered that this is now one of my favorite psalms. I think the word "law" threw me off. Only after researching the key words, did I realize the devotion and commitment that the psalmist expresses in this highly structured acrostic. I took the stanzas one by one and appreciated each one as a meditation on the word of God seen as Torah (instruction, direction, revelation). I then appreciated the message because of the commitment and love within the heart of the psalmist. It was through the careful scrutiny of the eight key words that I was able to see the bigger picture painted by the poet. Each of the words used shows the love he had for every facet of God's Torah to Israel.

Yet, I have just touched the surface of what the psalm is saying and what it means to a devout person who observes the commandments. Perhaps, this psalm was sung on the occasion of a pilgrimage to the Temple. If so, then an even greater experience of the love for God is lived through this work. Verse 54 is a fitting expression of this love: "Your statutes have been my songs wherever I make my home." For me the psalm was a "homecoming" found in the presence of the living personal God of Israel.

Psalm 120

This is classified as an individual lamentation. It is the first of a series of psalms called "songs of ascent." This classification is given as a superscription from psalms 120-34. These songs probably were sung by the Israelite pilgrims as they ascended towards Mount Zion and the Temple on the pilgrimage feasts of *Pesah*, *Shavuot*, and *Sukkot* (Passover, Feast of Weeks, and Feast of Booths). There is the possibility that they are also named after the 15 steps that were in the Temple and upon which the Levites sang the psalms while ascending them from the court of the women to that of the Israelites. A third interpretation is given to them because of the literary technique of parallelism and building up of an idea from use of the same word or words. This may be called synthetic parallelism which builds upon a thought, or climactic parallelism which builds upon a similar word, or emblematic which uses metaphors. There are some parts of the psalm that seem to fit these literary devices. This is especially seen in the verses where the liars and deceitful opponents of the poet are described (especially in verse 4) where the imagery is strikingly rich.

Psalm 120

The structure for the psalm is clear. Verses 1-2 are the introduction and the prayer of the psalmist which already has been answered by the Lord. Verses 3-4 are an imprecation in the form of a self-curse that the liars and deceivers bring upon themselves. Verses 5-7 form the lament of the poet and give the classification used for this psalm (an individual lamentation).

Reflecting on the content of this piece, we discover that the composer received an answer to his prayer for deliverance from the liars and deceitful persons. He goes on to show how these calumniators will undergo serious punishment similar to sharp arrows from a warrior who inflicts wounds upon them or to burning embers lit by the brushwood of which brooms are made. The poet finds himself to be like a lonely traveler or pilgrim who is trying to escape from hostile tribes from the north (Meshech) or from the bedouins from the desert in the south (Kedar). He calls himself a person of peace, while they are stubbornly rooted in being warmongers. Hoping to escape from such hostility, he yearns to make a pilgrimage to Jerusalem.

In my own spiritual battle for peace and tranquillity, I am often frustrated. This means that I find myself in a situation that does not seem to produce anything, and I cannot seem to do anything about this situation. The psalm reminds me that like the poet or psalmist, I can call out to God for deliverance and direction in how to relieve myself of the frustrating situation. Then I am led to search for a spiritual pilgrimage or journey of the heart. A walk in a park, a resting place near a river or brook, or a synagogue, church, or mosque may be the sacred space where I can vent my complaints to an all-merciful and personal God who not only hears me, but does so with a listening heart.

Psalm

121

🜍

This psalm is a pilgrim's prayer; it is classified by exegetes as a hymn of individual confidence. Similar in simplicity and structure to
the other "songs of ascent," its message is
clear and precise: God is ever present as a
guardian and a helper (savior).

The stair-like pattern used in these
psalms is easily detected in the repetition of
key words like helper (*'ezer*) and guardian (*shomer*). If we take
Mitchell Dahood's interpretation which is based on a Ugaritic
understanding of many of the words in the psalms, then several expressions in our psalm may be seen as titles for Yahweh
such as "mountain" in verse 1, guardian, shade, Most High, and
right hand. These titles show the protection and watchman-like
characteristics of God in the psalm. The Tetragrammaton
(*YHVH*) is used five times for "Lord" within the eight lines of
the poem. These multiple titles help the one reading or praying the psalm to focus on the central role that God plays in the
life of a pilgrim en route to the heights of Jerusalem as well as a
return home. God is seen as Creator and redeemer or helper
within the psalm.

The structure is as follows. Verses 1-2: The psalmist pro-
fesses his confidence and faith in God who is always present as
helper. Verses 3-4: The priest responding to this pilgrim
confirms that God is the guardian and protector of the person
either coming to the Temple or leaving after his pilgrimage.
Verses 5-6: This is constantly affirmed day and night. Verses
7-8: God defends the pilgrim always and everywhere on the
journey.

The contents of the psalm show that both the psalmist and
the priest who respond to his prayer assert this absolute trust
in God whose provident care is always manifested. This is
shown by the fact that both the coming and the going back home

are mentioned in the poem (verse 8). God is shown as Creator and savior and as the one who is there at the right of the pilgrim as shade for the sun and warmth from the coolness of night brought on by the moon. Creation is seen as ongoing through this protection of God who, unlike the other gods, never slumbers nor sleeps (verse 3).

I enjoy this psalm and I find it to be very consoling. The presence of God in every moment of my life in my "comings and goings" and in whatever I set out to do, is a constant within the eight lines of this little poem. It is a good reminder that God really is someone who cares about each of us who are created in the divine image and likeness. God as Creator and redeemer is present from our first breath to our last on this earth. The psalm is both an expression of our salvation history and of our origins from God. I was reminded while praying this psalm of my first visit to Israel. I had a profound emotional sense of awe and wonder as the plane moved over this land and came to the airport. I realize such experiences happen rarely in my life, but there have been a few for which I am thankful to the God of surprises. Such feelings are always remembered because of the intense quality of the event and its effect in one's life. Finally, I was reminded of line 73 of William Cullen Bryant's "Thanatopsis":

So live, that when thy summons comes to join,
The innumerable caravan, which moves
To that mysterious realm, where each shall take
His chamber in the silent halls of death,
Thou go not, like the quarry-slave at night,
Scourged to his dungeon, but, sustained and soothed
By an unfaltering trust, approach thy grave
Like one who wraps the drapery of his couch
About him, and lies down to pleasant dreams.

Psalm 122

This is considered a psalm or song of Zion. The word Zion is not mentioned in the composition, but Jerusalem is the city sometimes called Zion. Jerusalem is featured in this song. The joy of a pilgrim breaks forth in every line as he reaches either the beautiful city or the gates of it leading to the Temple. The song could also be his reflections upon the experience after he has returned home.

The structure of the poem is as follows. Verses 1-2: Joy in leaving on the pilgrimage and upon arriving near Jerusalem. Verses 3-4: The psalmist's admiration for the holy city. Verses 4b-5: The reason why Jerusalem is sacred to the pilgrim. Verses 6-7: Blessings and prayers for the holy site. Verses 8-9: Final blessing and an inclusion similar to verse 1.

Since this is a song of ascents, it fits the pilgrimage feasts well. Most consider it to be the Feast of Booths that is celebrated on this occasion, hence it would be an autumnal pilgrimage in thanksgiving for the harvest. It could equally be sung on the occasion of the Feast of the Unleavened Bread and Passover, or on the Feast of Weeks (*Shavuot*). These are the other pilgrimage feasts. Deuteronomy 16:16 reads: "Three times in a year shall all thy males appear before the Lord thy God in the place which he shall choose: in the feast of unleavened bread, and in the feast of weeks, and in the feast of tabernacles; and they shall not appear before the Lord empty."

The overall effect of the experience is breathtaking for the poet who sees the well-ordered approach of the tribes and the beauty of the buildings so wonderfully compact. He is ecstatic in his joy about this event which centers in Jerusalem both as a religious and sacred city as well as the seat of governance based on what great King David had established on Mount Zion. Particularly in verse six the poet carefully crafts his words to play on the similar sounds of peace, Jerusalem, petition, and prosperity in the Hebrew. The final lines are his prayer and blessing of the holy city and its inhabitants and, of course, his own friends and companions on the pilgrimage.

The study and praying of this psalm made me realize the importance of a gift that was given to me by the Dayton Christian-Jewish Dialogue a few years ago. It is a picture which has inside its golden frame a fresco from a synagogue at the top and another taken from a frieze in a church. At the center between these two designs is the verse in Hebrew and in Latin which reads: "For the sake of these my brothers and my friends, I shall say, 'Peace be within you'" (Psalm 122:8).

Psalm 123

This priceless little gem is classified as a hymn of confidence as well as an individual lamentation that becomes a communal lamentation. In reality it is a pure, simple prayer coming from the lips of one who is one of the "poor of Yahweh" (*'anavim/evyonim*). This servant of God puts all of his trust and confidence in God who is loving and tender in mercy. For the poor of the Lord such a prayer is the greatest act of surrender and trust in God.

There are only four verses in this psalm and the structure is clear. Verses 1-2: Address God through lifting of one's eyes to the heavenly throne; immediately the one praying invites the congregation to do the same. We notice a change from the singular to the plural in verses 1 and 2 respectively. Verses 3-4: The prayer begging for God's merciful kindness and protection against arrogant and scornful oppressors.

In the psalm both the eyes of the one praying and his voice

are apparent in this poem, helping the reader understand the importance of gestures and song in prayer. The imagery of eyes which are attentive to the hands of their master and their mistress is particularly striking and attractive. Every gesture is anticipated and carried out by the servants of the Lord. Both the service of the one praying and the graciousness of the benefactor, God, are seen in the simile, one of the most common and yet most beautiful in the Psalter. The prayer itself is presented in a simple, sincere, and reverent manner: "Be gracious unto us, O Lord, be gracious." The Latin version is devoutly expressed: *"Miserere nostri, Domine, miserere nostri."* The final verse gives the "case" or cause for the prayer. The poet and the people are oppressed and scorned by either their own rulers or, as is more likely, by the Samaritans. During the time of Nehemiah and Ezra the Samaritans attempted to prevent the people from rebuilding the walls of Jerusalem and the Temple.

As I read this psalm, I was reminded of an incident during a counseling session of a Lebanese person who told me how her father spoke very little during meals. He used only the gestures of his hand to tell the children when to pass something or eat or leave the table. The children followed his hand with great attention and with eyes wide open, knowing exactly his wishes. Surely, this down-to-earth imagery of the psalm arises from a home setting where the psalmist has his eyes turned toward the heavenly sanctuary or throne of God. He is convinced that only God can really help the situation of his people. And only God is the faithful benefactor who is both kind and merciful.

Arthur Weiser presents the idea of a kind father of a family who dishes out food while all eyes are fixed on the hand that conveys the gift. He says, "It expresses *reverential* awe, submission and humility, which are the result of the awareness of being utterly dependent on the sovereign will and power of God, as on the Lord with whom nobody can interfere; but it also expresses at the same time devoted love and trustful hope in the fatherly care that God as the Lord, will give his own. It is only when both these sentiments combine that the genuine attitude of prayer is achieved" (Weiser, 752-53).

Psalm 124

This is a thanksgiving hymn of the community of Israel. Like many of the other "songs of ascent" it probably was sung on the occasion of the pilgrimage feasts (Unleavened Bread-Passover, Weeks, and/or Booths). It definitely shows that it is a liturgical piece because of the invitation made directly to the congregation gathered at the Temple. During such a celebration the enthronement of *YHVH* as king had a central place in the festal worship of Israel.

Like most psalms, this one has no specific chronological information within it. It does seem to fit the time of Nehemiah when Sanballat, the Samaritan governor, was the oppressor both with word and deed. He continually harassed the people who were attempting to rebuild the walls of Jerusalem and the Temple. The psalm has been seen by others as referring to the Exodus in which the Israelites were delivered by the waters of both the Red Sea and the Jordan River. Other historical moments are suggested as well, for example, during the time of Sennacharib's besieging of the city of Jerusalem.

The structure is as follows. Verses 1-5: The direct call to Israel to affirm her trust in God as deliverer. Verses 6-8: Praise and thanksgiving to *YHVH* who is Israel's protector and deliverer.

This psalm, like the other "songs of ascent," has vivid examples, a certain stair-like construction between verses by the

use of repetition within the parallel lines, and a certain fresh-
ness and novelty about its development and structure.

Four striking examples are used for describing the perils
coming from the enemy and oppressors. First, their wrath is like
a burning and consuming fire approaching Israel. Secondly, waters are coming up to the neck (*nefesh* also means soul) of Israel
thus threatening her with death by drowning. Thirdly, Israel
is snatched from the "maw of the insatiable monster–death"
(M. Dahood, 3:212). Fourthly, the trap set for birds is vividly
painted, but happily, the snare or box-like trap with nets is broken and the bird quickly flutters into the sky with a fortunate
escape. I like Dahood's use of a Ugaritic parallel to show the
same vividness of the psalm: "Do not approach the son of the
god Mot [Death], lest he put you like a lamb in his mouth, lest
like a lambkin you be crushed by his grinding teeth" (Dahood,
3:213).

The thanksgiving prayer of the psalm starts with verse six
in praise of God who is the deliverer from all of the above dan-
gers. The last verse, eight, is a fitting conclusion still used in the
liturgies of synagogue and church. It also is a good reflective
verse on what the psalms are all about when it comes to the God
who acts in human history in favor of God's chosen people.

Recently, a friend of mine who is a liturgist, told me that
the last verse of this psalm is considered in monastic tradition
to be an antidote or remedy for sleepless nights when anxiety,
fear, doubts, and responsibilities invade our minds and hearts.
This is especially the case in the early hours before dawn when
one awakens and struggles with such thoughts. This verse is so
centered upon the God who protects us that it inspires
confidence in our prayer and then banishes the troubles like
wind blowing the clouds away. We finally, after tossing and
turning, realize it is best to pray the verse, "Our help is in the
Name of the Lord, who made heaven and earth." Amen.

Psalm
125
☙

This psalm has a mixed genre or type. It is considered a community song of confidence in God and a national lamentation. In the psalm we see that God is the protector of Israel just as Mount Zion and the mountains surrounding Jerusalem protect the sacred spot where David conquered the Jebusites and from then on the location was called Mount Zion. It was considered in the Hebrew tradition to be the center point of the earth; by going deep down into this site one would reach the origin of the womb of the earth. It has become a national symbol for Israel today. Jerusalem, therefore, is protected by God forever.

Verse three of the psalm shows the lament of the poet by describing the threat and tension that a foreign power has. This is seen in the symbolism of a scepter outstretched toward Jerusalem (see the sixth chapter of Nehemiah). Nehemiah was the appointed governor of Judea who set about rebuilding the walls and the Temple on Mount Zion. He experienced great opposition and harassments from the Samaritans under the leadership of Sanballat. The psalm continues with God being asked to keep the people secure and faithful. They who are just respond with an upright heart (a "listening heart," the constant theme of this present book). Those who are not faithful or the hostile nations turn onto crooked paths and God will lead them away. They are the enemy or the apostates.

Peace upon Israel! This last verse of the psalm leads me to pray for peace in Jerusalem, for this is a very sacred location for Jews, Muslims, and Christians. This psalm describes the tension we still feel when praying for Jerusalem and its inhabitants. After all, David, Mohammed, and Jesus are essential to the meaning and reality of Jerusalem as a sacred city. It is here that the three monotheistic religions have their roots in

Abraham, their father in faith. Perhaps, while the nation of Israel struggles with the quest for peace it is good for all believers to pray for the peace of Jerusalem, the Holy City. I was led to think of a line of poetry in "The Passing of Arthur" by Alfred Lord Tennyson:

> More things are wrought by prayer
> Than this world dreams of.
> Wherefore, let thy voice
> Rise like a fountain for me night and day.
>
> Book I, line 407

Psalm 126
℥

This is a community hymn of thanksgiving and lamentation. The psalmist creates another gem with this song easily adapted to a prayer of confidence and hope for the future.

The structure is easily seen as consisting of two strophes. Verses 1-3: Great joy at having returned to Zion after the captivity in Babylon. Verses 4-6: A prayer that the restoration of the good fortune of Israel will be brought to completion.

Like the other songs of ascent, this piece is simple and short. It contains catch words which are repeated in a stair-like development. The imagery of the similes depicts the joy and hope both now because of the return to the promised land, but also point hopefully to a successful future when all is restored. In a short topical inscription in the Vulgate translation we find a succinct summary of the psalm: *"Gratulatio de fine captivitatis; oratio ut perficiatur liberatio"* (joy or thanksgiving for the end of captivity; prayer that this deliverance may be perfected). Why such confidence? Because Israel centers its hope

on the person of the Lord (*YHVH*) who is invoked throughout
the ascent songs. There is also the mention of laughter and song
and smiling in the first strophe while tears and sadness are
turned to joy at the success of harvest time. Even the Gentile
nations say, "The Lord (*YHVH*) has done great things for this
people." Israel takes up that praise of God and sings its
Magnificat in this psalm. God has again acted in a marvelous
manner for the restoration of Zion and its people.

The metaphors used in the second part of the psalm are
enticing and attractive. Israel's hope is likened to the dried-up
wadis that are now filled with torrents of fresh clear waters. The
second metaphor shows the weary and tearful sower hopefully
strewing the seeds into dried-out furrows, but he returns at harvest time to find an abundant harvest. This leads us to think this
psalm was used for a harvest festival in Zion. It does have the
flavor and style of a post-exilic psalm.

During my years of study, I had the good fortune of living six months in Israel. As I researched and studied this psalm,
many of the scenes of the Land came back to me. I recalled the
kibbutzim in the north, the farms, the flowers. I thought of the
dried-up and arid Negev in the south, and then I thought of the
beautiful and elevated city of Jerusalem with its cool evenings.
The words of the psalm brought these scenes to life for me once
again and I thanked God for such an experience. Like the sower
who is hoping for the rains, I, too, yearn for a return to a peaceful land of Israel (*Ha-Arez*). At Passover these words are said
at the end of the celebration: "Next year... in Jerusalem!" (*Le-
shanah ha-ba'ah bi-yrushalayim*).

The mountain air is clear as wine, and the scent of pines
Is borne on the twilight breeze, with the sound of bells.
And in a slumber of tree and stone, captive to its dream,
Is the city that dwells alone — and in its heart a wall.

Yerushalayim of gold
And of copper and light,
Let me be a lyre
To all your songs.
(Taken from Naomi Shemer's famous Hebrew
hymn to Jerusalem found in Glinert, 259)

Psalm 127 ❦

This is a wisdom psalm. The superscription ascribes it to or by Solomon, the king who symbolizes wisdom. In the Hebrew the name Solomon received from David and Bathsheba was "Beloved" or *Yedidah* (2 Samuel 12:25) which appears in this poem, hence, reminding the reader of Solomon. Scholars do note, however, that this is by coincidence; the psalm is most likely post-exilic, written almost five hundred years later than Solomon.

There are two analogies in the poem which, in my estimation, are linked to one another. Both the building of a house and the development of a family are connected. The work of building a house for a home is similar to its purpose, that is, the beginning and development of a family within the home. The structure of the psalm bears this out. Verses 1-2: Building without the help of God is a vain endeavor. Verses 3-5: The gift of a family (sons and daughters) comes from God and with their growth, protection for the family at the city gates.

Within these songs of ascent, the repetition of certain words, the use of parallelism, and the colorful similes and analogies make of these songs a delightful literary experience. Their focus is on the providential care and presence of the Lord (*YHVH*); the poet is totally confident in God. A. Weiser says about this psalm that it shows "the decisive significance of God's actions in man's everyday life" (764).

From the background of Ugaritic, Mitchell Dahood sees a definite unity throughout the psalm both because of the alliteration in part one and a similar alliteration in part two of the piece. Thematic words and the content of the work also point to its unity.

I tend to agree with the Hebrew tradition of seeing this psalm fitting the time and history of Nehemiah when both the city walls and the Temple of Jerusalem were being restored. The reference to the family speaks of the repopulation so necessary during this moment in history for the people of Israel. Grown sons were necessary for the protection not only of the family but of the nation. This is symbolized by the reference to the city gates. This could equally apply to the settlement of internal problems where the gate represented a type of court of law.

My personal reflection takes me back to the tragic death of President John F. Kennedy (November 22, 1963). In one of the prayer services I heard this psalm being read as a prayer. In my further reading and research of the psalm, I was led to recall the mourning I went through. The lines seemed to fit the occasion for the event of such a tragedy affecting a nation losing its youthful leader. Each time I pray this psalm I think of President Kennedy and offer a prayer to God for his family. The psalm points out that God is essential towards helping us through the mysteries of suffering and of dying.

Psalm 128

🙃

This literary gem is a companion wisdom psalm to Psalm 127. It emphasizes the positive blessing upon a person who is reverent and devout in keeping God as the center of his life. Like Psalm 1 this person keeps the precepts and laws with joy. The Torah is a holy way of life for the blessed one. The psalm achieves this positive perspective by developing similes that are connected with family life. The father, the mother as wife, children, and the home are all to be found in the verses of this song. It happens to be one of the rare occasions where we actually envision children happily seated at table in a peaceful home (see likewise, Zechariah 8:5). The structure for the psalm is as follows. Verse 1: The happiness of the one keeping the laws and precepts of the Torah. Verses 2-4: A change in the personal pronoun occurs emphasizing the direct praise of one who experiences the good fortunes of a healthy and prosperous family. Verses 5-6: The priest or Levite confers a blessing upon the family and the nation.

This is a psalm which "presents a beautiful cameo picture of an ideal home life" (Cohen, 430). Such happiness reflects upon the security of the people and nation of Israel in their fidelity to God; peace is the result and blessings are received. The themes of the psalm are so well balanced that the reader experiences delight with this artistic and literary gem. Parallel similes strengthen the overall wisdom genre of the piece which focuses on a specific subject, the family. This positive picture is quite refreshing and offers a more sanguine complement to Psalm 127.

In reflecting and praying this psalm, I am remembering my experience of celebrating the Passover Haggadah with a family in the holy city of Jerusalem. All of the descriptions of this psalm come to life again and I relive that beautiful experience. Even the youngest member of the family had a role to play in this celebration as he asked the question, "Why is this night so different from all other nights?" The rest of the family and guests listened to the greatest liberation story ever told — the Exodus. They actually were reliving that event with songs and food and drink to celebrate God's mighty act for the people Israel. I was fortunate to have celebrated the feast in the Holy City with a prosperous and blessed family. The psalm describes what I saw in that gathering. Today I pray for the peace of Israel by praying Psalm 128.

Psalm
129
☙

This psalm has several classifications by the commentators (exegetes). It is considered to be a community lamentation, a psalm of confidence of the community, and a communal thanksgiving. The same ambiguity about its provenance (origin) and date reigns among the scholars from pre-exilic to post-exilic, etc. My personal impression and appreciation of the psalm is that of a lamentation stemming from an "I" psalm that is then personified in the people of Israel who take up the theme of the psalm through a response. Dahood proposes the best analysis for the structure of the psalm by breaking it into two parts. Verses 1-3: The priest or psalmist recalls and laments the past oppressions endured by Israel in Egypt. Verses 4-8: The imprecation or plea of the sufferers against the oppressors.

The psalm is about salvation history wrought in favor of Israel all the while recalling the beatings and slavery endured by the people. They seemed to be trampled upon and furrows were beat into the backs of the people of Israel, yet God brought them through this harrowing experience. They now are going to ascend to Mount Zion and climb the steps to the Temple singing of their past plight and asking God to wreak havoc on their oppressors. This is especially seen in the second part of the psalm, verses 4-8, where Dahood gives a brilliant explanation of verse 4 as being part of the imprecation. His translation captures his insight on the mode used in imprecations (the jussive or optative): "May Yahweh the Just snap the yoke of the wicked." This is an excellent lead-in for the rest of the psalm fitting the plea of the sufferer Israel. Two similes are used: the enemy is like grass which quickly flourishes on a rooftop, but withers by evening since there are no roots; or like the reaper who cuts the grass with a scythe in his right hand while grasping the useless grass in his left and throwing it aside. Thus when others come by the field they see no need to ask for a blessing upon such a bad patch. The reader understands that the true blessing redounds upon Israel.

The ascent songs are thought to be processional psalms for the ascent up to Jerusalem, then up to Mount Zion and finally the steps of the Temple. The feast of the booths (*Sukkot*) is probably the occasion for the psalm. I find that the background for the feast helps me experience and appreciate the emotions and pleas of this poem. The words of Leviticus 23:42-44 are a good background for the feast and, in my estimation, for the psalm: "Ye shall dwell in booths seven days; all that are Israelites born shall dwell in booths; that your generations may know that I made the children of Israel to dwell in booths, when I brought them out of the land of Egypt: I am the Lord your God. And Moses declared unto the children of Israel the feasts of the Lord."

Psalm 130

☌

This psalm is an individual lamentation. It is one of the most spiritual expressions of a penitent seeking the forgiveness of God (*YHVH*, *Yah*, and *Adonai*). Martin Luther considered this one of his favorite psalms and he added it to the psalms from citations mentioned in Paul's letters which he considered to be the best (Psalms 32, 51, 130, and 143). This psalm, 130, was considered in early Christian tradition to be among the seven "penitential psalms" (6, 32, 38, 51, 102, 130, and 143). I consider the psalm to be structured into two movements. Verses 1-4: A penitent calls out to God for forgiveness and God does forgive. Verses 5-8: The psalmist calls out to Israel to do the same and Israel receives forgiveness and redemption.

We experience a perfect way of praying for forgiveness through the psalm both because of its personal dimension of contrition from a faithful and open heart and also for the confidence this person has in God who is all-merciful and forgiving (*hesed*). We are, as readers, given a positive image of God and can readily identify with the desire for reconciliation with the Lord our God. God's forgiveness is all-encompassing in this poem. God's attentive ear is bent towards the penitent who has a listening and contrite heart. The poet has a profound respect and awe for the Lord God that liberates him from the depths of the abyss of death and the watery jaws of Sheol, the region of the dead.

Attentiveness is a striking feature of this psalm. We see this in the repeated verbs: to hope for, to wait for, to watch even through the night. The hope and repentance of the psalmist is paralleled by the merciful and loving-kindness of the God who redeems Israel and forgives this penitent. The psalmist turns towards the congregation of Israel encouraging the people to have the same contrite disposition of heart and the same confidence in God the Redeemer.

There are two unique areas in the psalm. The first is the similarity of the phrase "let Thine ears be attentive" to what is found in Nehemiah 1:6. This may suggest that the psalm comes from the period of time from 458 to 428 B.C.E. The second unusual word is the word for forgiveness (*selichah*). Mitchell Dahood states, "The root of the rare noun selichah, 'forgiveness' (v. 4), occurs in the divine attribute *sallah*, 'forgiving,' a hapax legomenon in Ps. xxxvi 5" (3:235)." By *hapax legomenon*, Dahood means that it appears only once in the text of the Hebrew Bible.

In my personal reflecting upon this moving psalm, I am reminded of my participation on one occasion in a synagogue for the service called *Selichot*. Prayers for forgiveness are offered during this special evening of prayer. One of my friends had a list of his "sins" which he brought and prayed for their forgiveness on this occasion. I was deeply moved by his disposition and attentiveness to God who forgives our sins. I discovered that *Selichot* takes place before the Jewish New Year (*Rosh Hashanah*) and is a season of repentance continuing up to the Day of Atonement (*Yom Kippur*). The next time I attend *Selichot*, I will make sure to bring along a copy of Psalm 130.

Psalm
131
🜩

This is a psalm of individual confidence and trust in the Lord. It happens to be one of the beautiful gems of the Psalter even though it is the third shortest one after Psalms 117 and 134. There is a deep spiritual dimension to these shorter psalms. This particular one describes perfectly the attitude and spiritual disposition of one of the poor of *YHVH*
(*'anavim*). These are the people who put absolute trust in God realizing that only God is able to guide and comfort them. The psalmist uses the touching imagery of a babe in its mother's lap and arms — probably a weaned child nearing three years of life. There is a splendid insight into true tranquillity, peace, and comfort from such a picture. The psalmist has through fidelity and experience reached an age of mature integration and contentment with his life thus recalling the days when his mother held him and the same feelings were there. Now the poet is centered upon God with great trust and affection. He addresses God directly and leaves aside all proud thoughts and looks; he no longer meddles in things or ideas beyond his comprehension.

The Soncino commentary takes us into the heart of the imagery expressed in the phrase "like a weaned child." It reads: "A remarkable piece of imagery. An infant in its mother's arms instinctively yearns for her milk; but after being weaned, it still finds happy security when held by her although the earlier longing has passed. Such is the psalmist's condition after weaning himself from the desire for prominence" (Cohen, 435).

In the conclusion of the psalm, the composer turns to the congregation of Israel and invites the people to have a similar experience of trust and love towards the Lord (*YHVH*).

All of us can take ourselves back to such an experience of childhood and we smile about the peace and joy we experienced in our mother's arms. We still are moved with joy whenever we see a mother holding her child with tender love and affection. Perhaps, the rabbi who wanted to teach his students about true happiness in life used this psalm as an example. He was not getting the right answer from them. Finally, he has to tell them that true happiness and blessedness in life comes to those who are content with their lot in life. The great theologian and bishop of Carthage, Augustine, began his personal life story called *Confessions* with the following sentence: "The heart is restless till it rests in Thee, O Lord." In Isaiah we hear the Lord saying, "As one whom his mother comforts, so will I comfort you, and ye shall be comforted in Jerusalem" (Isaiah 66:13). And, "Can a woman forget her nursing child, that she should not have compassion on the son of her womb? Yea, they may forget, yet will I not forget thee" (Isaiah 49:15).

Psalm 132

This is a royal psalm; it belongs with the following group of royal psalms: 2, 18, 20, 21, 45, 72, 101, 110, and 144. These psalms center on *YHVH* and his anointed, David. Some of these psalms are considered royal messianic songs. Though they may not all come from the monarchic golden age of David and Solomon, they do apply to the promises made to God's anointed ones in the lineage of David, the kings of Judah.

Psalm 132 is also listed among the songs of ascent used in the procession up to Jerusalem and to the dwelling place of God in David's city of Zion (Jerusalem). The psalm fits well with the period in which Solomon (961-922 B.C.E), David's successor, set about building the Temple in Jerusalem.

The psalm consists of two complementary parts which

194

probably were used for the festival of the enthronement of *YHVH* once the Temple was built. *YHVH*, David, the ark of the covenant, and Zion are interconnected throughout the psalm thus giving it a literary unity.

The following structure results:

Part I: Verses 1-10 which may be divided as follows. Verses 1-5: David's vow to build a dwelling place for *YHVH*. Verses 6-7: The pilgrims sing while the ark is discovered and brought up to Jerusalem. Verses 8-10: The liturgical prayers offered in the preferred sacred place of Zion.

Part II: Verses 11-18: God responds to the fidelity of David the servant king and promises perpetuity to the Davidic line provided the covenant is observed.

This processional song centers on a sacred re-enactment of the events of David's desire to build a place for the presence of God, then on the discovery of the ark of the covenant at Kiriat-yearim (Forest-village), and finally on the celebration surrounding the ark once it is brought to Zion. Though David is not the builder, his name is remembered because of his role in making Jerusalem the center of the formal confederation of the twelve tribes. This was a strategic religious as well as political decision that did unite the tribes of the north and the south. David's concern and ardent devotion is carried out by Solomon his son whose history really begins with the construction of the Temple in Jerusalem (1 Kings 5-7).

In the use of the psalm for the covenant festival of *YHVH* as king the psalm continues in use for the procession in the years after Solomon. Thus the celebration is not bound to one historical moment but is a living re-enactment showing the experience of the people and the king and priests in the festival. God's presence is experienced anew in each epoch and is just as real as the first event. The liturgical atmosphere, the singing, and the offerings are what make this celebration real again and again.

In the second part of the psalm, *YHVH* is responding to David's desire and devotion as king. Many of the words and themes from part one are remembered. For example, verse 16 corresponds to verse 9, verses 17-18 to verse 10. God's fidelity is experienced in the promises made in the past whenever the king and the people are faithful to the covenant. There are also parallels seen in the historical books of the *Tanakh*, 1 and 2 Samuel, 1 Kings. There is a similar theme in Psalm 89 which, however, is later and contains lamentations, and 2 Chronicles 6:41 takes verses 8-10 from Psalm 132. Salvation history, liturgical celebration, and devotion are essential to this song.

On the door inside my office and study I have a dark green banner that I inherited from a friend who worked and studied in Jerusalem. The banner celebrates David as king and comes from the traditional site of his tomb near the western wall of the Temple. It reads: "In praising him — David — may there be peace upon us and upon Israel." The banner reminds me of several of the ascent psalms but this one in particular is remembered. In thinking about the western wall I am led to prayerful thoughts and fond memories from the past when I spent six months in Jerusalem.

Psalm 133

Although this is classified by most exegetes as a wisdom psalm, the ascent songs have a unique inventiveness about them. The original thought of the composers to call them ascent songs is appropriate for the journey up to the Temple in Jerusalem on festive occasions. Castellino, in his monumental commentary calls this psalm together with Psalms 121, 123, 126, and 134 as varied prayer songs (*Preghiere*

Varie). Wisdom sayings in Hebrew are expressed by the word *mashal* which embraces many forms such as similes, parables, sayings, riddles, proverbs, oracles, and a practical example for a specific need. It could well be that the purpose of this psalm is the desire for national and family unity during a time when this was threatened either externally or internally in Israel. The similes used in verses two and three are meant to demonstrate how blessed it is to be united under *YHVH*, the one true God. The occasion of a pilgrimage to the sacred shrine of the ark of the covenant in the Temple would spur the author to create such a hymn for the twelve tribes of Israel. They were united under David and Solomon; those were the golden years of the monarchy. Why not be united now as brothers and sisters in Jerusalem?

The similes used describe the strength, comfort and beauty seen in a unified people under the kingship of God. The sacred oil running down the high priest's beard is a powerful symbol of unity. The length of Aaron's beard indicates his honorable and dignified role — whether it is the oil that touches the opening at the neck of his garment or his beard that falls over its collar — both are part of the polyvalent meaning of the *mashal*. The oil brings consecration to the priest under Aaron's name, cleansing and healing, and exudes with the fragrance of blossoms. The second simile based on a proverbial statement about the dew of Mount Hermon contains the same meaning. This dew refreshes, enriches, and develops growth within the parched ground below the slopes of the mountain. So, too, will unity under *YHVH* allow peace, prosperity, and unity to fall upon the tribes of Israel. These are blessings desired from God.

Konrad Schaefer concludes his commentary on this psalm saying, "On Mount Zion and in the liturgy personal and ideological differences which threaten to destroy group identity, submit to the confession of one God. The poem anticipates the harmony of all people as they live without defenses in God's creation whose care for all is a continually unfolding blessing" (316).

In the Dayton Christian-Jewish Dialogue, one of the members is an excellent cantor for the group. On special occasions he passionately and devoutly sings this psalm in Hebrew with its magnificent tones and sounds. The melody is catching and exhilarating for the Dialogue participants who always open with a "devotion." I am reminded of the Latin version of the psalm which is put into a lively chant and is sung on special occasions such as the closing of a spiritual retreat for the religious congregation or on the occasion of the celebration of vows lived for twenty-five, fifty, sixty, or even seventy years. Whether on the occasion of a Dialogue meeting or a jubilee, and whether sung in Latin or Hebrew, I am sure the original composer would have seen the purpose of his song achieved. Yes, how good and how pleasant it is when brothers and sisters gather to praise and thank God for blessings bestowed on them.

Psalm 134

This liturgical psalm is the final song of the ascent songs. It is a call to praise and bless the Lord who is the maker of heaven and earth. This takes place in the night when the priests and Levites continued the praise and blessing of God while the people return home. The psalm is the second shortest in the Psalter; it is a beautiful conclusion for the set of 14 psalms of ascent (120-34).

The psalm may be interpreted and translated in several ways. The faithful of Israel who have journeyed up to Jerusalem may be the ones called to praise the Lord (*YHVH*). "Servants of the Lord" is used for all of the faithful of the congregation or for faithful Israel. The expression may be referring to the priests and Levites who are summoned to continue praying and blessing God throughout the night. Or it may be the priest sending the pilgrims home with a blessing from God for their own welfare.

The psalm centers on the Lord (*YHVH*) mentioning the divine name five times! Each of the three verses contains the Tetragrammaton divine name *YHVH*. In my interpretation I see the priests and Levites being called upon to bless and worship the Lord who is the Creator of heaven and earth. Thus verse one and verse three are a literary inclusion. The psalm centers on God the Creator as seen in Genesis 1-3. M. Dahood, in his unique, inventive manner, sees as a possible translation "works of the Lord" instead of servants of the Lord and this would also confirm verse one and three with a literary inclusion. In verse two the expressive gesture of raising one's hands to the sanctuary or to the heavens seems to indicate a priestly gesture of spreading the fingers of the hand while praising and blessing God. The possibility of there being a "change of guard" among the Levites and priests would enable the prayers to continue throughout the three customary watches of the night characteristic of Hebrew thought. The priests or one of them could also be sending the pilgrims home with God returning and reciprocating their praise and blessing. The pronoun used in verse three is second person singular which could mean either the congregation of Israel as a whole or each one individually receiving a blessing for having made the pilgrimage to Zion.

My personal reflection on this psalm led me to think about the tribe of Levi. It did not have any particular land assigned to it. Levi belonged to the Lord and his inheritance was the Lord and the sacred places and things of the Lord. I was impressed with the following citations mentioned by scholars in the study of this psalm. In Deuteronomy 10:8: "At that time the Lord set apart the tribe of Levi to carry the ark of the covenant of the Lord, to stand before the Lord to minister to him, and to bless in his name, to this day." And in 1 Chronicles: "In addition, there were the singers, the heads of Levitical families, who were accommodated in the Temple, free of other responsibilities because they were on duty day and night." And for the blessing mentioned in verse 3, see Numbers 6:24-26: "May the Lord bless you and guard you; may the Lord make his face to shine on you and be gracious to you; may the Lord look kindly on you and give you peace."

Psalm 135 ❦

This hymn praises God the Creator and the redeemer of Israel. Though some would say the psalm is a pastiche or anthological song composed from other parts of the Scriptures and psalms, the hymn itself is carefully structured and has a comprehensive message of God both as Creator and Savior. The election of Israel is part of its message. There is a remarkable development within the hymn that synthesizes the marvels of creation and the wondrous and miraculous presence of God in the Exodus and the conquest of the promised land. The entire *Tanakh* (Hebrew Scriptures) creates the background for the poem. Scholars have easily found similarities to the Torah, the Prophets, and the Writings within its verses.

I discovered that Konrad Schaefer's analysis of the psalm and its two panels of creation and salvation for an elected people to be helpful in my own reflections upon this hymn. He presents the following chiastic outline for the psalm:

Psalm 135

A. Hallelujah! (Praise the Lord)
  B. Invitation (vv. 1-3)
    C. Election of the people (v. 4)
      D. God's superiority (v. 5, cf. Ps 95:3)
        E. God's universal authority (vv. 6-7)

        E/ God's past action on behalf of the elect (vv. 8-12)
      D/ God's unsurpassing renown (v. 13).
    C/ benefice to the people (v.1 4)
        F/ nothingness of the idols and idolaters (vv. 15-18)
  B/Invitation (vv. 19-21)
A/ Hallelujah (Praise the Lord)

(Schaefer, 317).

We are not forced to regard the psalm as lacking in originality because of its dependence on other psalms. Weiser says, "This fact is to be accounted for by the psalmist's deliberate adherence to the fixed and stylized forms of tradition which had their place in the cultus" (788-89). Affinities are seen between Psalm 135 and its neighbor 134 (God as Creator in verse 3). There is also a reversal of the order in the opening lines with Psalm 113. Verses 15-18 are seen in Psalm 115:4-8; Psalm 95 is reflected in its verse 3 and verse 5 from our Psalm 135. And verses 8-12 match what is found in Psalm 136:10-22. The mosaic created by such similarities is part of psalm tradition in the liturgy of the Temple.

The psalm is framed by an Hallelujah at the beginning and one at the end (an inclusion of verse 1 and verse 21). The exhortation to sing and praise the Lord is found in verses 1-4. The final verse (4) of the first strophe contains a good insight into how God's predilection for Israel stems from the covenant. The word *segullah* means God's special treasured possession similar to a precious jewel. The word is found in the Torah in three places: Exodus 19:5-6 (Covenant and Decalogue): "Now, therefore if ye will harken unto my voice indeed, and keep my covenant, then ye shall be My own *treasure* from among all peoples; for all the earth is mine and ye shall be unto me a kingdom of priests and a holy nation." In Deuteronomy 7:6-7 we see that the love of God is the reason why Israel is a chosen, precious treasure: "For thou art a holy people unto the Lord thy God; the Lord thy God has chosen thee to be his own *treasure* out of all the peoples that are upon the face of the earth... because the Lord loved you (v. 8)!"

In the continuing verses of the poem the redemption of Israel is seen in the mighty acts performed by God against Pharaoh and his firstborn both of man and beast and in the conquering of Sihon and Og, the kings of Canaan. Israel thus enters the promised land (verses 8-14).

The song makes sport of the bogus gods of the nations (Gentiles), reducing them and their makers to nothingness or inanimate creatures. Finally, there is the universal exhortation to continue praising and blessing God. Israel, the house of Aaron, the Levites, and all the devotees of *YHVH* are part of the chorus that ends with a sonorous and grand "Hallelujah."

In my personal reflection upon this psalm, I realized that it contains a healthy theology since it touches upon creation and redemption. On this point both Jews and Christians are in agreement and can use this psalm with their understanding of it from two different religious perspectives. The great intellectual giant of the Middle Ages, Thomas Aquinas, constructed his *Summa Theologica* on the words Creation and Redemption.

Psalm
136
❧

This is the famous Great Hallel, a liturgical hymn for the Passover celebration. It has a repetitive antiphon for the latter part of each of its 26 verses: "for his loving-kindness endures forever." This is the response of the congregation to the invitation and the chanting of the themes by a Levite or a priest, perhaps even by a choir of Levites in the Temple. It may be compared to a praying or singing of a litany. Its rhythmic quality brings a certain focus and continuity to the themes contained within the song, namely, creation, salvation history, and divine providence. The psalm covers all times up to the present pilgrims who have come up for one of the three great feasts.

The structure of the psalm agreed upon by most commentators is the following. Verses 1-3: The cantor's invitation to the congregation to praise and thank God. Verses 4-9: God's loving-kindness is extolled in nature seen in God's creation (cf. Genesis 1). Verses 10-22: God is always present during the Exodus and the Conquest of the Land. Verses 23-26: God is always there for the lowly; God's providential care extends to all the pilgrims.

The word *ḥesed* appears in all of the verses. This definitely is at the heart of this psalm and despite the many translations offered for the word, the one that I prefer is loving-kindness. *Ḥesed* is associated with the enduring covenant that God made with Moses and the people of Israel at Sinai. This *ḥesed* occurs 245 times within the *Tanakh* (Hebrew Scriptures) and 127 times within the collection of psalms. It is, so to speak, at the heart of the psalms and one of the most important thematic words in Scripture when it comes to understanding the love of God as a person. In covenantal contexts it is coupled with the qualities of faithfulness and loyalty. As a refrain in our psalm we see similarities in Psalms 105:1 and 118:1-4. One of the keys towards understanding *hesed* is the text of Exodus 34:6 which is background for many of the psalms: "The Lord, the Lord, a merciful and gracious God, slow to anger and rich in kindness and fidelity."

Our hymn has resonances to Genesis 1 as seen in verses 5-9; then of Exodus in verses 10-22. Similar to its sister Psalm 135, it takes up the themes of creation and redemption which are characteristic of historical psalms. There is also the element of thanksgiving in such a psalm.

The liturgical nature of the psalm and its traditional expressions make it ideal for the pilgrims coming up to Jerusalem for one of the three great pilgrimage festivals. The long pilgrimage matches the continuous remembrances of the journey that God has made with the devotees as they make their way to Mount Zion in Jerusalem. The pilgrims relive the experiences of their ancestors through the ever present God of creation and history. Especially significant is verse 23 where the present generation is meant: "The Lord remembered us in our misery, God's love endures forever." In a marvelous concluding verse the chant returns to the opening invitation with a sonorous praise and thanksgiving to God and a clamorous Hallelujah.

The Great Hallel (Psalm 136) is recited at the Passover after the little Hallel (Psalms 113-18). "The custom originated in Temple times when Hallel was recited during the offering of the pilgrims' sacrifices on Passover Eve, while the paschal lambs were being slaughtered, and again that night when they were eaten during the Seder" (Werblowsky and Wigoder, 170).

Psalm 136 is a very helpful type of prayer whenever we are at a loss for words or thoughts about God. This litany-like hymn helps us center on the greatest of God's attributes, (*hesed*) God's loving-kindness. The word *hesed* may be a mantra for us when we are weary and unable to concentrate on prayer.

Through *ḥesed* we are brought back to the presence of God. This is the purpose of Psalm 136: the praise and thanksgiving to God for the loving-kindness we experience. Hallelujah!

Psalm
137

☙

This psalm is a community lamentation. It is the most poignant and violent of psalms in its expressions of blind rage and passion against the Babylonian captors and the Edomite ravagers of the holy city of Jerusalem. Verse 9 is one of the most oppressive verses in all of the psalms: "Blest is he who seizes and dashes your infants against the rock." Rather than censor or bowdlerize the words we should see them in the context of the effects of war, violence, and terrorism heaped upon an innocent people. Today's wars of genocide, violence and terrorism do summon up such sentiments among the persons without much religion or education. Neither men, women, children or babies are spared when it comes to terrorism. Feelings become raw and passionate when one's own family has been the ones attacked and killed. Mitchell Dahood correctly interprets the plain meaning of verse 9: "Thus those exegetes who interpret verse 9, 'your infants,' as the adult citizens depicted as the children of Mother Babylon will scarcely convince the critics conversant with the curses of the eighth century B.C. *Sefire.* Inscription in Aramaic" (3:269).

As a lamentation, verses 1-6 are among the saddest in expressions and images. They are coming from the soul of a person who is mourning and weeping upon being asked to do just the opposite — to sing joyful songs about Zion. This psalmist is either speaking from his firsthand experience of the Exile or, in a flashback to that event, recalling how the personal tragedy of living in an unholy land affects him even after returning to Zion. There he experiences further sorrow at the city which has been raped and devastated by both the Babylonians and the Edomites, the dreaded neighbor enemy of Israel.

Despite the rage and uncontrollable passion seen in this psalm, it is one of the most carefully constructed in its contrasts and literary devices. Dahood makes clear his appreciation for the poetic quality of this paradoxical psalm: "The language of the sixth century lament is marked by originality and vividness. One encounters assonance (vss. 1-6), alliteration (vss. 3, 8), two word plays (vss. 5, 9), vocative *lamed* (vss. 7), double-duty suffix (vs. 7), the use of the independent personal pronoun as the direct object (vss. 1, 6) and a word with double entendre (vs. 7b)" (3:269).

The structure of the psalm consists of three strophes. Verses 1-3: The remembering of the biting requests of the Babylonians to sing psalms of Zion. Verses 4-6: The great passionate love for Zion prevents the Israelites from singing psalms in Babylon. Verses 7-9: The curse imprecations against the Edomites and the Babylonians for the rape of Zion and Jerusalem.

The city of Babylon is noted for its great rivers: the Tigris, the Euphrates, and the Chebar. There were also numerous canals from these rivers. Upon being asked in a taunting and inane manner to sing about Zion, the psalmist hangs up his harp on the tree and would rather have his right hand be forgotten so that he cannot play the harp and that his tongue would be paralyzed and muted so that he could not sing a song in an unholy land for these scoffers and taunters.

His words, perhaps, are now a song among the ruins of Jerusalem and becomes a curse against the Edomites who sacked the city after the Babylonians had broken down its walls and driven the Israelites into the land of Babylon. This curse is so strong that it is censored in liturgical use today.

Almost every spiritual commentary on the psalms treats of the difficult curse psalms within the Psalter. Dahood's remark above is to be kept in mind. Perhaps, C.S. Lewis' solution for them was to allegorize the enemy Babylon and Edom as the seven capital vices which are like tiny serpents within the human heart. He encourages the spiritual person to crush these "infants" in spite of their moans and whimpers. This helps the person who is inclined to moralize and spiritualize the cursings. This is evident in patristic commentaries on the psalms (e.g., in Origen and Jerome). We have to understand the curse psalms in the light of the following note in the Soncino commentary on verse 9 of the psalm: "Perhaps, if some of their modern critics had been under the yoke from which the psalmist had been delivered, they would have understood a little better how a good man of that age could rejoice that Babylon was fallen and all its race extirpated" (Cohen, 448).

Psalm 138 ❦

This is a psalm of individual thanksgiving. It may be the king acting in the name of the whole community who offers this song of praise and thanksgiving in the Temple. If so, it may then be classified as a royal psalm of thanksgiving similar to Psalms 81, 92, and 144. This is quite different from an exilic hymn such as Psalm 137 for it is offered in the sanctuary of the Temple and there are expressions of confidence rather than lamentation within it. The fact that the Temple is mentioned lends credence to the idea that this may be offered by one of the kings of Judah, perhaps during the time after Solomon 900-800 B.C.E. Mitchell Dahood, who has unique and credible insights into the psalms favors such an interpretation.

The structure of the psalm agreed upon by many commentators is as follows. Verses 1-3: A definite concrete act of thanksgiving and praise offered in the Temple. Verses 4-6: A prayerful wish on the part of the psalmist or king that other kings would also be led to offer praise and thanksgiving to God. Verses 7-8: Confidence in the divine protection of God and prayer that the work of the king or psalmist be accomplished.

Throughout the psalm three key words are used; God is called Lord (*YHVH*) seven times; thanksgiving or *todah* is the theme of the psalm; covenantal fidelity and love from the Lord toward Israel is emphasized (*ḥesed*). The first stanza thanks and praises the Lord for having delivered Israel. The Lord is above all other gods claimed by the nations (cf. v. 4). The king thanks and praises God with all his heart and soul in response to the divine *ḥesed* of the Lord. The king's sentiments are similar to those found in the great prayer of Deuteronomy: "Hear, O Israel, the Lord our God is one Lord; and thou shalt love the Lord thy God with all thy heart, and with all thy soul, and with all thy might" (Deuteronomy 6:4-5). The second stanza is the prayerful desire of the king who prays that all other kings and nations will come to praise and thank God as he does. God's words are fulfilled and the Lord is concerned about the lowly while keeping the haughty away from such concern. In the third stanza, we find a thought similar to the great Psalm 23, namely, that the king will not fear walking in the valley of tribulation. He is confident that the Lord will protect him and see the works of his hands accomplished.

Konrad Schaefer has a splendid insight to this psalm in his concluding paragraph: "All of life is the work of God's hands; may he who began it sustain it forever (v. 8). Because God fulfills his purpose, because the divine *ḥesed* is unending, to abandon the work of his hands would be a denial of the self. The recognition of 'your *hesed*, O Lord, endures forever' is all the confidence a person needs" (325).

I personally was helped to pray this psalm by the use of three words within it: Lord (*YHVH*), thanksgiving (*todah*), and loving-kindness (*hesed*). The title for Lord (*YHVH*) which is used seven times in the middle and end of the psalm shows me the God-centeredness that my prayer should have. It offsets any consideration of others taking the place of God as verse 1 and verse 4 indicate about the gods of the nations. Yahweh or Lord is present 695 times in the Psalter or about ten percent of its appearance in the *Tanakh* (Hebrew Bible). The total use in number is 6,828 times. This is the preferred way of addressing God in the Psalter. It is based on the theophany Moses experienced on Mount Horeb (Sinai) when he saw the burning bush and was told to remove his sandals for he was on holy ground. Where I choose to pray may be likened to the holy ground. In Psalm 138 it is the sanctuary of the Temple wherein the ark of the covenant lies. In reflecting on the word *hesed* or the loving-kindness of God, I am led to feel the warmth of God's protection around me. As I ponder over this presence and protection of God, I am led to pray similarly to Psalm 138. This then is another Hallelujah experience.

Psalm 139

This profound psalm is classified as a wisdom psalm. If we understand biblical wisdom as the placing of God and God's will above all other persons and concerns, then this psalm is a remarkable reflection and prayer coming from an innocent person who possesses wisdom. The relationship between the poet and God is an intimate one expressed in I-Thou terms. The psalmist poet contemplates the omniscience, the omnipresence, and the omnipotence of God the Creator. As a composition this piece touches existence as profoundly as any other psalm in the Psalter. It makes sense to us today because of its personalism and its wisdom.

The psalm is a literary unit which may be divided as follows. Verses 1-6: God knows all things. God's omniscience is presented and admired with ardor and wonder. Verses 7-12: God's presence is everywhere and the poet extols this presence. Verses 13-18: An astounding reflection on the forming of the poet from the first moment of his existence — even from his mother's womb. Verses 19-24: The innocence of the poet and his renunciation of those who have judged him unjustly. God is the ultimate and infallible judge.

The psalm is pre-exilic (that is before 587-586 B.C.E.). The prophet Amos cites parts of it; so, too, does Jeremiah and Job. The scholar W. Holladay attests to the earlier dating by noting that Jeremiah uses a verse of the psalm in an ironic manner. He notes that sarcasm is not a characteristic of the Psalms; it is Jeremiah who is sarcastic (41). Please note the above references: Amos 9:2-3; Jeremiah 23:23-24; Job 17:13.

The opening six verses describing God's knowledge is well written in the poet's use of verbs and nouns of knowing. His own uncanny way of speaking about the knowledge of God is in absolute contrast with what God knows. Konrad Schaefer notes some of the words which are framed with the beginning of the psalm such as "search," "know," "discern," and the noun, "thoughts" (325). Paradoxically, the psalmist is sensed as fearing the hemming in and the constraints that the knowledge of God puts upon him, yet he is ecstatic about this experience. This leads him to further describe God's very presence in verses 7-12.

In the second stanza the language of contrasts and parallel thought continue wherein all space is inundated with the presence of a personal God. There is a silent monologue going on within the poet's own heart where he listens to the voice of God. This brings about a sense of wonder in the psalmist. In a colorful metaphor characteristic even of Homer, he expresses dawn as having wings: "If I take the wings of the morning and dwell in the uttermost parts of the sea; even there would Thy hand lead me, and Thy right hand would hold me." In the Hebrew Soncino commentary this is noted: "To the ancients (Semites, Greeks, Romans, etc.) the goddess of the dawn had wings with which she arose out of the Eastern ocean, and, in the course of the day, covered the whole sky. The psalmist makes a happy use of this imagery, without in the least compromising his monotheism" (Cohen, 452, citing Wilton Davies).

The third stanza describes God's wondrous work in human creation. Here the deepest insight and reflection about the dignity and mystery of human life is expressed. God has knit together the inmost parts of the poet within the womb of his mother. From both the secrets of mother earth at creation and from the realization of the span of human life seen in God's book of life, the poet wonders and contemplates the mystery of his own life coming from the hands of the Creator. In wondrous awe he realizes how God's thoughts are greater in number than the grains of sands on the seashore (verses 17-18).

The final verses of the psalm are rather abrupt. Here the justification of the psalmist's innocence is proclaimed over against the idolaters and the evildoers. It is likely that the poet is clearing his reputation in front of God's judgment seat from the false accusations against him. Far from the scurrilous declarations of his enemies is his own sublime testimony that he has described in his prayer and poem.

This psalm becomes a contemplative experience for me each time I read it. It helps me appreciate the wonder and mystery of God's wisdom. The poet's own divinely inspired praise leads me to ponder the mystery of human life and creation. In a recent decision, I opted to make a retreat away from the busy things I do each day. This would enable me to enter into the heart of this psalm and have those intense moments of prayer that are necessary for an I-Thou relationship with God, my Creator. I came back from the experience of the retreat with an act of thanksgiving for the gift of life that I enjoy from my Creator. This psalm will always have a preferential treatment in my more contemplative moments of prayer.

Psalm 140 ೪

This psalm is an individual lamentation. It has linguistic traces of an early northern Semitic influence and therefore is most likely pre-exilic. Words in the psalm appear only here, the so-called *hapax legomenon* (Latin for "to be read once"). There is evidence of a chiastic word order and also a *casus pendens* in the stanzas. The piece is easily broken into five stanzas because of the word Selah (probably a pause in the singing or recitation of the psalm); this word occurs three times in the poem, making it easy to have five stanzas. The stanzas are as follows. Verses 1-4: The superscription uses the word leader or director for the song for the last time in the Psalter; it is also attributed to David. In this stanza the psalmist prays for deliverance from the serpentine tongues of slanderers. Verses 5-6: The enemy or slanderer is compared to a hunter setting traps and nets. Verses 7-9: *YHVH* is addressed and asked for protection. Verses 10-12: Imprecations that the plans of the malefactors be reversed. Verses 13-14: Those dependent on the Lord will certainly be vindicated.

Psalm 140

This poem is a literary unit with excellent use of the chiastic word structure and the characteristic parallel thought of Hebrew poetry. The imagery is rich and colorful. Konrad Schaefer points out these literary devices in the psalm (329-30). The enemies are described as having serpent tongues and are likened to all the crafty tricks of a hunter. Verse four is especially masterful in Hebrew with the hissing sibilant sounds of the snake.

In the poem, God is called upon ten times; seven times the sacred name *YHVH* is used for God, then *El*, the exalted one, then finally the reverential word *Shem* or Name. Such a preponderance of the names for God attests to the absolute confidence and profound faith of the psalmist who knows where his help has its source. The imprecation or curse elements in the psalm ask God to reverse what is being done to an innocent person. This creates a tension for the reader of today, but is a release and deliverance for the innocent one. The poem results in a confirmation that God does care and gives providential surveillance for the "poor of *YHVH*" or those who have no one else to defend them except God.

In my personal reflection, I am led to think of one of the cruelest forms of prejudice, especially in anti-Semitism through the use of stereotyping and caricaturing and making sport of a Jewish person or of the people of Israel. In Christian-Jewish dialogue this is one of the first steps to become aware of and to make efforts to remedy them in whatever circumstances one hears these cutting remarks. The hurt from such remarks frequently causes the Jewish person to remember the Shoah (the Holocaust). Pain shoots through the heart and memory of the victims of these prejudicial and harmful words. Through dialogue one becomes sensitive to such an offense and to the untruth connected with it. We are to take steps to confront those who use anti-Semitic language both in conscious and unconscious fash-

213

ion. Unfortunately, it is frequently heard in one's own family and among one's friends. The courage that our psalmist expresses in prayer is needed for us in stepping up and confronting the offenders. Their tongues are as biting as the serpent's fangs and as harmful as the venom of the snake.

Psalm 141

This poem is a lamentation of an individual who invokes the Lord (*YHVH*) to preserve him from the temptations offered to him by wicked people. The structure is as follows. Verses 1-2: The prayer of the psalmist is like incense offered at the evening sacrifice. Verses 3-6: A wisdom motif and concerns about sins of speech the opposite of his prayer. Verses 7-10: God's justice convicts the evildoers and is a help for the psalmist.

In this song we see the power of prayer in the face of difficult and strong temptations coming from the example of others. The psalmist's struggles are intense and searing because of the sweet attractiveness and yet the biting cunning of the unjust leaders or judges. The personal prayer of the poet is offered during the evening service in the Temple, for his gestures are those used in this offering, namely, the lifting up of his hands to the sanctuary. Mitchell Dahood, with his characteristic inventiveness posits a reasonable scenario: "The lament of an Israelite living in the North Israelite dispersion after the fall of Samaria in 721 B.C.E. Brought to trial for having refused to participate in pagan rites (vs. 4b) and banquets (vss. 4d and 5c), the psalmist, in the first stanza prays to God to guard his lips lest he abjure his Yahwist faith and to punish him severely should he partake of heathen banquets" (Dahood, 3:309).

The text is quite difficult because of corruption or lacunae in verses 5-7, but it is evident that the one praying is wrestling with temptations dealing with pagan worship. It is the desire of the psalmist to overcome these evil customs of speech and idolatry. Perhaps, this colorful translation of verse 6 is right on target: "Let their judges drop into the clutches of the Crag, and let them hear how dulcet are his words" (Dahood, 3:308).

For me, the heart of this psalm is found in the first four verses while the latter part consists in the obstacles and temptations from which the poet is asking God to deliver him. His final prayers are an act of confidence that God will help him escape the traps and nets of the hunters.

I find that the thick description of the temptations expressed in this psalm demonstrates that things always seem greener on the other side, but through prayer and discernment, we can be persons of wisdom who want to do God's will. We are led to see in these attractive inclinations that they do not produce good results in our hearts and souls. Deep down we find out through our prayer that they are not real to what counts for a wholesome way of life. We know that it is only through prayer, such as the one expressed in our psalm, that we realize how unwise it would be to give in to these temptations. Oscar Wilde's solution is not negotiable, namely, "The best way to get rid of a temptation is to give in." Like the psalmist, our direct trust in God and our sincere prayer is part of the answer. Moreover, we realize we have to live with the consequences of our decisions in these matters. Only God can help us escape the traps, nets, and gains of such attractive temptations.

Psalm
142

🎶

This plea for help from an individual is classified as a lamentation psalm. The superscription calls it a *maskil,* a term which occurs fourteen times within the Psalter. The meaning springs from the radical *s-k-l* and refers to skill, artistry, and intelligence. The Levites are often the ones who hand down the psalms to us along with these notes about the music and spirit of the psalm. In 2 Chronicles 30:21-22 we have this information about the Levites: "The Levites and priests praised the Lord day by day, singing with loud instruments unto the Lord... the Levites who taught the good knowledge of the Lord."

Arthur Weiser point out that this psalm offers the reader a perfect model for what an individual lamentation entails. Verses 1-3a: The customary introduction with an invocation and an expression of trust in the Lord. Verses 3b-5: The lamentation proper or the reason why the poet cries out for help. Verses 6-7: The petition for deliverance accompanied with thanksgiving, anticipating the divine assistance which results in the psalmist joining the community of the faithful who trust in the Lord.

Such a psalm comes from one who may be called one of the "poor of *YHVH*," that is, one of the *'anavim* who depend on God who alone can help and deliver such a person. It is the absolute trust and dependence that the person already senses which is fulfilled and thus accompanied by an act of thanksgiving within the prayer. The Levites and priests had no land; their only heritage was to be possessed by God and dedicated to God. They are said in the psalm "to dwell in the land of the living," an expression which indicates total dependence on God.

K. Schaefer sums up the psalm in this manner: "The path of life is a prison from which there is no escape. God is the only relief and the only worthwhile portion in the land of the living" (333).

After the death of my mother, I remember praying in the spirit and mode of this psalm. Tragedy had broken out around me in several areas of my life and work. Even a friend was incarcerated and pressure was put upon me to seek his freedom. Then another dear friend decided to cut off all contact with me. I was devastated and felt alone in all of these events. My emotions and spirit were at an all-time low. I consulted with a spiritual advisor thereby hoping to share these burdens but without any resolve. It was only in the silence of listening with my heart to the words of this type of prayer that I was able to surrender myself to God in these things that I could not control by myself. God did bring me through after some length of time and I was able not to give in to anger or severe depression. I had become one of the "poor of *YHVH*."

Psalm 143

This psalm is an individual lamentation with similarities to Psalm 142. In it we have images of impending death, a courtroom judgment, and cultic prayer. Both H. Gunkel and M. Dahood have argued for separate compositions in verses 1-6 and verses 7-12; the themes and style of the psalm appear to be from the same composer. Likewise, two important thematic words frame the psalm: servant of God (*'eved*) and God's loving-kindness (*ḥesed*).

Both parts of the psalm have paralleled structures which are seen as two movements within the same piece. I prefer to keep the traditional unity of the composition as the one to work with in my brief commentary on this psalm. Verses 1-2: A perfect invocation showing absolute trust in God for deliverance. Verses 3-6: The afflicted one gives a description of the case or situation. Verses 7-9: Repeated appeals for God's assistance. Verses 10-12: Confidence and thanksgiving that the request will be heard.

The psalm may be seen in two ways. First it could be the king who is making the appeal to God for help. The psalm then would be pre-exilic. Or the psalm may come from the lips of an ardent and devout Levite who is connected with a northern shrine and is using the song in his act of worship. This would explain the expression "before the face of the Lord" and the prayerful gesture of raising one's hands to the sanctuary. In verse five, a difficult verse because of the state of the text, I find there are verbs which show prayer in various modalities. For example, remembering connected with hope; meditating on God's work in creation; and musing or pondering over, thereby illustrating a reflective prayer mode. These modalities are seen in cultic prayer connected with a sacred place; in cultic tradition, history whether personal or that of the community becomes salvific (*Heilsgeschichte*).

The contrasts in this poem are striking. We see death, the nether world or Sheol, and judgment on the one hand (verses 2, 3, 4, 7b, 9, 11b) and, on the other hand, great hope, prayerful examples, confidence in God, bold invocation, trust in God's loving-kindness (*ḥesed*) and docility (verses 1, 5, 6, 7a, 8, and 10). Verse 12 shows the ultimate purpose of the psalm through the hopeful resolution of the situation because of God's goodness, mercy, justice and truth.

Despite the dark images of death and judgment, hope and trust on the part of the poet lead him to walk on level ground. His heart is open and listening to the Lord. The Lord is to teach him God's will. His pleas and requests are definitely going to be heard and answered. The litany-like progression is rich in imagery and expression.

I personally found this psalm helpful for my own prayer. I find the psalmist to be a person of profound and varied forms of prayer which are both cultic and communitarian as well as individual. His gestures, his inner attitude seen in the powerful verbs used for his modes of prayer show that God is the one who acts for the sake of the individual and the community in a salvific manner. Affliction, judgment and pain are here, but hope and awareness of the presence of God carries this psalm from the poet's heart to my heart with its emotions. I especially like the unique request made upon God, "Teach me to do Thy will, for Thou art my God; let Thy good spirit lead me in an even land" (verse 10). See also the parallels to Deuteronomy 4:43 and Psalm 26:12.

Psalm 144

This is a royal psalm. Despite some Aramaisms in its composition, the song has pre-exilic traits. We sense the era of the earlier times of the kings of Judah who live under the glory and mantle of David who had skill as a warrior and as a singer of psalms. In this psalm we can see the king praying for God's blessings upon the people of Judah. Rather than saying that the psalmist has borrowed from other psalms, I see the author using traditional phrases found in the liturgical practices and cult of the Temple. There are traces of several genres of psalms in the composition which I think is characteristic of traditional worship in the Temple.

My structural analysis reveals the following: Verses 1-2:

A blessing and praise of God by a king; several of God's attributes are present in this invocation. Verses 3-4: A hymn of wonder about creation of human beings. Verses 5-8: A theophany with prayers for deliverance. Verses 9-11: The thanksgiving of the psalmist. Verses 12-15: Prayer for national safety and wholesomeness coupled with a sapiential blessing.

The suppliant is a king who describes how God has given him the skills of a successful warrior over his enemies. God is his rock, his tower, the merciful one, the fortress, deliverer and shield, and the victor over enemies both within and without his territory. The king realizes his limits and is humble and aware of God as Creator in many wondrous ways. The king recalls the theophany of Sinai and asks God to display such power and glory again. He recalls how David was the first royal psalmist and now this king strikes up a new song; convinced victory is assured, he thanks God for it. As sovereign the king is concerned for his people and thanks God for the virile young men and the stately maidens. He thanks God for the prosperous flocks, the abundant fruits of the harvest, and the grain and food. His song ends with a double blessing issuing from the mouth of the priest in the Temple: "Happy is the people that is in such a case, yea, happy is the people whose God is the Lord" (verse 15).

In my personal reflection on this psalm, I resonated with its use in the synagogue. The Soncino commentary notes, "In the Jewish liturgy it prefaces the service for the termination of the Sabbath (Prayer Book, 210). 'The praise of God as the One *who traineth my hands for war and my fingers for battle*' fits well with the imminent renewal of the weekday struggle; after the Sabbath calm comes the intrusion of the world, against which the psalm proceeds to invoke God's protecting hand; while the joys of a full garner and an overflowing sheepfold are those to be attained by the labour which is once more man's lot.... But,

as the psalmist continues, whatever comes to man in his warfare is of God's doing. It is from Him that man wins the power
to triumph and the fruits of victory. Prosperity is only real when
this is recognized" (Abrahams, cited in Cohen, 464).

Psalm
145
⚕

This is a remarkable hymn of praise and is
among the most positive psalms in the
Psalter. It was composed by an individual
who probably called it a "prayer"; it is so
called in the manuscript on the psalms discovered at the Dead Sea. It is an acrostic
psalm following the letters of the Hebrew alphabet like other acrostic psalms (25, 34, 37,
111, 112, 119). This is the only psalm that has the inscription
"A psalm (prayer)" using the word *tehillah*. The plural form of
this word is the Hebrew for designating the entire Psalter,
namely, *Tehillim*.

The use of an acrostic does put restrictions on a composer,
but this psalm is remarkable in its originality, its warmth of expression, and its sensitive religious piety. Add to this the quality of universalism, and you have another feature of its literary
beauty.

In the psalm numerous names and appellatives are given
to God who is given due glory in practically every line of the
song. It serves as an interlude between the last of the so named
Davidic psalms in Book V (Psalms 138-45) and the great concluding Hallel or Hallelujah psalms (146-50) which brings the
Psalter to a conclusion that is similar to a musical orchestration
or fanfare of sound and message. God is extolled fourteen times
in this psalm and the universal dimension is seen in the use of
the word "all" which appears ten times within the composition.

Since this is an alphabetical psalm, I consider the succeeding lines of the Hebrew alphabet as the structure for the poetic piece. The stanzas may be seen by means of the change of voice from I to Thou to a third person. There is also a fascinating mystery to the psalm for it lacks the letter *nun* or "n" in its composition; however, several of the versions of this psalm like the Septuagint, the Vulgate, and the Syriac include a verse for this letter of the alphabet. This is attested to in the Dead Sea Scrolls manuscript on the inspired psalms (11 Q Ps (a) XVII, 2-3): "Faithful is God in his words, and merciful in all his deeds." The same manuscript adds another lovely dimension to the song by having a continued response of "Blessed be *YHVH*, and blessed be his name forever." Thus we may have a "litany of sacred names" (3:335).

I personally was edified by the following citation from an unidentified rabbi who says, "Another rabbi declared: Whoever recites this psalm thrice daily may be assured that he is a son of the World to Come, because it contains the verse, 'Thou openest Thy hand and satisfiest every living thing with favour,' i.e., an acknowledgment of man's dependence upon God's grace. In conformity with this teaching the psalm occurs three times in the Jewish liturgy for every day (Prayer Book, 29, 71, 94). This psalm inaugurates the concluding group which rounds up the Psalter with a series of hymns of praise, reaching its climax in the superb Hallelujah of Psalm 150" (Cohen, 467).

222

Psalm
146

℘

This hymn of praise begins the series of five concluding hallelujah psalms. The word hallelujah says what these psalms are all about: "Praise the Lord." The simplicity of Psalm 146 is unique in its absolute trust in the Lord. God's name as *YHVH* or its abbreviated form *Yah* appears eleven times, then as *Elohim* twice, and finally as *El* once. Thus a double use of the sacred number seven showing fullness and completeness in the praise and reverence due to the holy name of God. Such a psalm then is totally centered on God. There is a symmetrical pattern of presentation in which God as Creator is seen in the first half of the song, then God as Redeemer in the second part. The background for the composition seems to be Genesis 1 and Exodus 22, respectively.

The psalm is likewise very positive with the exception cautioning the faithful not to trust in princes or those in high places. There is an imprecation against those who are wicked (see verses 3-4, 9b). Striking are the benevolent and kind acts of God seen in verses 7-9: God effects justice for the oppressed; gives bread to the hungry, opens the eyes of the blind, raises up the bowed down, protects strangers, orphans, and widows; and loves the faithful ones or the *zaddiqim*. All are the so-called *'anavim* or poor of *YHVH*. They have only God to trust absolutely.

This psalm expresses beautifully the faith of Israel who as a people realize that "God keeps faith forever" (verse 6c).

The psalm starts with a magnificent opening in which God's sacred name is invoked four times. The superscription is hallelujah which is also the concluding note of the song. Throughout the rest of the psalm one can easily see the parallelism so characteristic of Hebrew poetry and the symmetry of the total composition in its parts. The mention of Zion alerts us to the summoning of the whole community of Israel on the occasion of a festival honoring the kingship of the Lord.

In summary the psalmist is inviting us to praise the Lord (verses 1-2) while showing it is worthless to trust in humans (verses 3-4). God, however, is absolutely trustworthy in all of our trials and crises (verses 5-10). This is so because God is Creator and Redeemer in the flow of salvation history for Israel's faithful ones. God reigns forever.

I am reminded of a story my mother told me about my grandmother, Anna. She managed a small boarding house for immigrants who worked in the steel mills of Pennsylvania. Polish and Slovak men and their families were served meals and given rooms. Mother helped in the cleaning and serving. Grandmother also had worked in several Jewish homes and had upon returning home shared this with my mother. She said, "Helen, if you really want to learn how to pray then you must pray as the Jewish people pray. They really know how to pray." I treasure this reminiscence that my mother shared with me and thought of it at the end of my research on this particular psalm. In praying the psalms, especially the hymns of praise, I realize that I am immersed in the heart of what it means to pray. Prayers of praise are equivalent to saying many times during the day and night to God, "I love You." This form of prayer is not petitioning or thanking God for favors. It is simply expressing our love of God. This I think is what the psalms are trying to do. It is only with our listening hearts that we are able to praise God with our voices. If we are not able to do this with our own thoughts and words, then we have these wonderful hallelujah psalms to open our hearts and praise God.

Psalm

147

♉

This is a community hymn of praise. The Hebrew text (Masoretic) presents this piece as a unity, but several versions break it into two psalms, namely, the Septuagint Greek, the Vulgate Latin, and the Syriac: Psalm 146:1-11; Psalm 147:12-20. I prefer in this commentary to keep the Hebrew intact since that is the canonical text for the synagogue. It is a liturgical hymn of praise used in the Temple with three distinct movements within the psalm. Verses 1-6 praise the Lord as the restorer of Jerusalem and Israel. This is seen in a history that is salvific *(Heilsgeschichte)*. The second movement is seen in verses 7-11 in which God is praised for divine governance over all of nature. And the final movement is seen in verses 12-20 where God's word is effective in bringing about peace and prosperity for Israel through the revelatory word of God. The psalm is framed with an opening hallelujah and a closing one. Verses 2 and 19 are framed with the reference to Israel. Thus three themes appear in this song, namely, praising God, thanking God for Jerusalem and Israel, and finally the theme of God's revelation through the word of God. All of these aspects of the psalm are appropriate in a liturgical celebration during the harvest time in Israel. We see this in the effects of God's power in nature represented by rain, snow, ice, frost and the harvest.

As is evident in most of the hallelujah psalms, God's name is extolled. In this psalm the name of God appears seven times, again a number of completeness. The praise of God is considered to be sweet and pleasant as a prayer; this is unique within the Psalter and is a gentle liturgical persuasion for summoning Israel to delight in praising God. Another sensitive touch and beautiful image is found in verse 9 wherein God pays attention to the cry of the ravens and then feeds them: "He giveth to the beast his food, and to the young ravens which cry" (verse 9).

A number of years ago in the city of Dayton, the synagogue of Temple Israel sponsored a concert in which the psalms were featured. Both traditional and modern renditions were heard by the congregation. Most of the hymns were songs of praise similar to Psalm 147. The music coupled with the revealed words of God in these psalms was a pleasant and joyous experience for the listeners. This truly was a pleasant prayerful evening in which God was praised.

Psalm 148
☙

This is another magnificent hallelujah hymn praising God the Creator. It is based on the Genesis creation story in chapters 1-2:4a, which probably owes its origin to a priest of the Temple. The spirit of the psalm captures the Genesis story which is the opening chapter of the Torah. God's nature is expressed through the Hebrew word *Shem* (Name), which is a reverent way of talking about God. Then all of creation is summoned to praise the Name.

Konrad Schaefer (342) gives us a splendid insight through a structural analysis of the symmetry of the psalm:

Hallelujah
invitation to the heavens, "Praise the Lord (seven times)
  v. 5a "Let them praise the Name of the Lord
  three phase motive: he commanded, established,
    fixed (vv. 5b-6)
invitation to the earth, "Praise the Lord (once)
  v. 13a, "Let them praise the Name of the Lord"
  three part motive: exalted Name, glory, people
    (vv. 13b-14a)
Hallelujah

Psalm 148

I prefer the following outline or structure proposed by Mitchell Dahood as a complement to the observations of Schaefer. Both commentators helped me understand the word order and composition of this wonderful hymn in praise of God and God's creation. Dahood says, "It is remarkable for its tripartite structure, evidently modeled on the motif distinguishing three categories of beings" (3:352).

Verses 1-6: Addresses the heavenly beings to praise the Name of God.

Verse 7: A unique verse which invokes the netherworld to praise God.

Verses 8-13: The terrestrial world is summoned to praise the Creator.

Verses 13c-14: A conclusion to the poem consisting of a reflection on the relationship of the God of the universe to the people of Israel.

By examining the Genesis narrative and the deutero-canonical (apocryphal) excerpt found in Daniel 3:52-90, the psalm is cited in parts. To me this posits the writing of Psalm 148 between the seventh and third century B.C.E.

Again like the final psalms of the Psalter, this hymn begins and ends with a hallelujah. These praises of the Lord enclose the marvels of God's creation throughout the body of the psalm. Verses 1-5 summon the heavens, the angelic hosts, the waters above the heavens, then the sun, moon, stars (and planets, according to Dahood). Verse 6 proclaims that God established, confirmed, and commanded their orderly existence, therefore praise is due to the Creator. Verse 7 then summons the netherworld with its mythic deeps and sea monsters to praise God. Verses 8-12 call upon the earthly creations both animate and inanimate as well as the hierarchy of rational humankind to praise God. Verse 13 offers us the reason for giving this praise. Verse 14 then is the conclusion which also is a lead-in to Psalm 149. Thus the psalm is a rhapsody sung by all of creation blending their respective harmonic sounds in a jubilant and majestic praise of God the Creator.

My personal reflective prayer took me back to the beautiful creation narrative of Genesis 1:1-2:4a (Priestly tradition). I meditated on the seven days of creation realizing that the narrative itself is not enough for a prayer of praise. Then turning to Psalm 148 I discover that creation and praise are blended into the song of prayer. I am led through the verses to praise God for all of the gifts of creation. I am challenged to respect the ordinances and laws of nature with reverence, awe, wonder, and care. I conclude my prayer with the great ending of our Psalm 148, a majestic Hallelujah.

Psalm

149

🎗

This hallelujah psalm is a communal hymn of triumph. It is not able to be assigned to a specific time or era. Commentators range from pre-exilic times to the time of the Maccabees (around 135-104 B.C.E.). The hymn is appropriate for the celebration of the enthronement of God as king over Israel, thus it pertains more to a theocracy. Again we notice that it begins with a hallelujah and ends with one. It affirms that God is the person who elects, rules, loves, and grants Israel victory over the enemy whomsoever that may be.

Verses 1-5 demonstrate the centrality of God in this liturgical festive hymn. Singing a new song, rejoicing, dancing, and playing the full array of musical instruments adds great zest to the opening stanza of the psalm. Verses 6-9 proclaim God's triumph over all nations and peoples. This will be a final and complete victory of God. Israel is God's assembly of devoted and holy ones. They are the children of Zion who sing the new song in praise of *YHVH*. God's judgment and verdict, written down in the book (verse 9), "alludes to the destruction of the pagan nation of Canaan, the accomplishment of which had continually been made the religious duty of the people of Israel (cf. Deuteronomy 7:1ff; 20:13)" (Dahood, 3:357).

Konrad Schaefer makes an interesting comment in comparing Psalm 2 with Psalm 149: "As the second to the last psalm in the Psalter, Psalm 149 corresponds to the location of Psalm 2, which announces that through the royal Messiah God will claim rulers and nations. In Psalm 149 the human instrument is the assembly of the faithful, who function as a messianic community through whom God achieves what was assigned to the Davidic king" (345).

In these days of violence and terrorism, even religion can be a source of violence and terror for those who are fanatics. Slogans coming from sacred texts are used to bolster violence and terror. Expressions like "God is on our side" or "Praise the Lord and pass the ammunition" were used in previous world wars. We sense similar tendencies in some areas of the world today. Perhaps such slogans are not used, but the motivation from religion drives certain religious-minded people to acts of violence even to suicide bombings. The psalms are meant to be prayers and are interpreted as such in this book which is an attempt to listen to these inspired prayers with a *lev shome'a*, that is, with a listening heart. Only when we are in tune with the God of peace and love are we able to sound the depths of these prayers. We know that we need to move beyond some of the harsh words of the psalmist because of the many years of experiencing the prayer mode of the psalms. It is people who are the humble ones before God or today's "poor of *YHVH*" who have this openness to the deeper meaning of prayer as expressed in the Psalter. For such people the psalms then take on the quality of singing a new song to the Lord which hopefully others will learn how to listen to with their hearts. It is only when we pray the psalms in sincere praise of God that we will experience the peace of God no matter to which nation we belong.

Psalm

150

This musical hymn of praise is the grand finale of the Book of Psalms. It is a jubilant symphony of praise beginning and ending with Hallelujah. In fact, the whole psalm may be designated as one grand Hallelujah. Carroll Stuhlmueller says it so well: "The final word of the entire Psalter is Hallelujah! Just as the other four books within the Psalter concluded with a solemn doxology (Pss 43:13; 72:18-[20]; 89:52; 106:48), the curtain is rung down on the entire Book of Psalms with a super-solemn call to praise, an entire Psalm 150" (221). Oesterly calls Psalm 150 "the grandest symphony of praise to God ever composed on earth" (cited in Cohen, 479).

Here is the structure I suggest for the psalm: Verse 1-2: The invitation to praise the Lord (Hallelujah); verses 3-5: Praise God with every possible musical instrument and with dance; verse 6: The great call to all of creation to a thunderous Hallelujah!

The opening verse shows us that God is in the heavens or in the heavenly sanctuary. In verse 2 this is confirmed by the synonymous parallelism of the Hebrew text. It is the dwelling place of God, the heavens. The praise is an imperative used ten times: "Praise ye, *YHVH!*" Apparently the Levites and choir take this command seriously for there is a response seen in the ten forms of musical appreciation of the summons. The instruments are the trumpet, psaltery, harp, stringed instruments, timbrel, two types of cymbals, the human voice, and finally an expression of music in the dance. Do you remember David dancing before the ark? All of this is a splendid picture of an orchestra harmoniously praising the Lord in the Temple. This is what psalms are all about: "A heartbeat of life and worship." All of creation is called to praise God; all that has breath (Genesis 1:27).

Psalm 1 (verse a:1) began by telling us who is really a happy and blessed person. Now as the Book of Psalms comes to a close we hear a jubilant Hallelujah. The bookends are now in place for the rest of the Psalter which calls out to listening hearts. We are to take up the human response contained in these vibrant and energetic prayers which contain many of the human experiences and emotions we have in our lives. As Maclaren states about our final psalm, "The Psalm is more than an artistic close to the Psalter; it is a prophecy of the last result of a devout life"... and let everyone sing out, "Hallelujah!"

P.S. The Theodulphian manuscript of St. Jerome reads: "The Psalter is complete; there are 2,527 verses."

References

Anderson, G.W. "The Psalms." In *Peake's Commentary on the Bible*. London: Thomas Nelson & Sons, 1964.

Boadt, L. *Reading the Old Testament: An Introduction*. New York, NY: Paulist Press, 1984.

Bruggemann, Walter. *Message of the Psalms: A Theological Commentary*. Augsburg Old Testament Studies. Minneapolis, MN: Augsburg, 1984.

Bullough, Sebastian, O.P. "The Psalms." In *A New Catholic Commentary on Holy Scripture*. New York, NY: Thomas Nelson, Inc., 1975.

Castellino, D. Georgio, S.D.B. *Libre dei Salmi*. Roma: Marietta, 1965.

Clifford, Richard J. "Psalms." In *Collegeville Commentary* #22-23. Collegeville, MN: Liturgical Press, 1986.

Cohen, A., ed. *The Psalms*. London: The Soncino Press, 1969.

Dahood, Mitchell. *Anchor Bible: Psalms*. 3 vols. Garden City, NY: Doubleday, 1970.

Dollen, Charles. *Prayer Book of the King: The Psalms*. Staten Island, NY: Alba House, 1997.

Fuller, Reginald C., ed. *New Catholic Commentary on Holy Scripture*. London: Thomas Nelson and Sons Ltd., 1975.

Glinert, Lewis. *The Joys of Hebrew*. New York: Oxford University Press, 1992.

Holladay, William L. *The Psalms through Three Thousand Years: Prayerbook of a Cloud of Witnesses*. Minneapolis, MN: Fortress Press, 1993.

Jenecko, Benedict, O.S.B. *The Psalms: Heartbeat of Life and Worship*. St. Meinrad, IN: St. Meinrad Archabbey, 1986.

233

Kselman, J.S. and M.L. Barré. "Psalms." In *The New Jerome Biblical Commentary*. Englewood Cliffs, NJ: Prentice Hall, 1990.

Lamb, J.A. *The Psalms in Christian Worship*. London: Faith Press, 1962.

Lewis, C.S. *Reflections on the Psalms*. London: G. Bles, 1958.

MacKenzie, R.A.F., S.J. *The Book of Psalms, Old Testament Reading Guide 23*. Collegeville, MN: Liturgical Press, 1967.

Mowinckel, Sigmund. *The Psalms in Israel's Worship*. New York and Nashville, TN: Abingdon, 1962.

Murphy, Roland E., O.Carm. *Responses to 101 Questions on the Psalms and Other Writings*. Mahwah, NJ: Paulist Press, 1994.

Prévost, Jean-Pierre. *A Short Dictionary of the Psalms*. Collegeville, MN: Liturgical Press, 1997.

Sabourin, Leopold, S.J. *The Psalms: Their Origin and Meaning*. Staten Island, NY: Alba House, 1974.

Sacred Writings: Judaism, The Tanakh. The New JPS translation. New York, NY: Jewish Publication Society, 1985.

Schaefer, Konrad. *Psalms: Studies in Hebrew Narrative and Poetry*. Berit Olam. Collegeville, MN: Liturgical Press, 2001.

Siegel, Danny. "A Blessing." In *The Lord Is a Whisper at Midnight*. London: Town House Press, 1985.

Stuhlmueller, Carroll. *Psalms 2*. Wilmington, DE: Michael Glazier, Inc., 1983.

Weiser, Arthur. *The Psalms. Old Testament Library (Commentary)*. Philadelphia, PA: Westminster Press, 1962.

Werblowsky, R.J. and Geoffrey Wigoder, eds. *Encyclopedia of the Jewish Religion*. Jerusalem-Tel Aviv: Massada-P.E.C. Press Ltd., 1966.